Here's what people who should know say about Doro[t]

Make the Most of Your Best

"Today's world calls upon business executives to articulate their views in a variety of forums. Dorothy Sarnoff identifies a person's speaking strengths, builds a framework of confidence around those strengths, and completes the picture of a credible spokesperson with a flourish. Indeed, she makes the most of your best."

—John F. Bookout
President and CEO
Shell Oil Company

"Begin this book and you won't put it down. An exciting learning experience for anyone wishing to improve his communications with others." *—Richard Voell*
President
Penn Central Corporation

"Anyone who has watched Dorothy Sarnoff in action has experienced, as I have, a master teacher who draws the best out of everyone around her. This excellent book is bound to increase the number of those who have benefited from the Sarnoff approach in putting across spoken messages."

—Edward Wakin, Ph.D.
Professor of Communications
Fordham University

"From the standpoint of anyone who has had to speak before an audience, Dorothy Sarnoff provides wonderful guideposts to enhance the process of effective communications."

—Arthur Levitt, Jr.
Chairman
American Stock Exchange

"I have seen Dorothy Sarnoff turn dozens of tongue-tied executives into spell-binders. This book explains how she does it."

—David Ogilvy
Creative Director
Ogilvy and Mather International

Books by Dorothy Sarnoff

MAKE THE MOST OF YOUR BEST
SPEECH CAN CHANGE YOUR LIFE

Make the Most of Your Best

A Complete Program
for Presenting Yourself
and Your Ideas
with Confidence and Authority

By Dorothy Sarnoff

An Owl Book

HOLT, RINEHART AND WINSTON
NEW YORK

Copyright © 1970, 1981 by Dorothy Sarnoff

All rights reserved, including the right to reproduce this
book or portions thereof in any form.
Published by Holt, Rinehart and Winston,
383 Madison Avenue, New York, New York 10017.
Published simultaneously in Canada by Holt, Rinehart and
Winston of Canada, Limited.

Library of Congress Cataloging in Publication Data
Sarnoff, Dorothy.
Make the most of your best.
"An Owl book."
Bibliography: p.
Includes index.
1. Oral communication.   I. Title.
P95.S27   1983   001.54'2   82-11927
ISBN 0-03-062376-6 (pbk.)

First published in hardcover by Doubleday & Company, Inc.
in 1981

First Owl Book Edition—1983

Printed in the United States of America
10 9 8 7 6 5 4 3 2 1

Grateful acknowledgment is made to the following for permission to reprint
their copyrighted material.
   Lyrics from the song "I Whistle a Happy Tune," by Richard Rodgers
and Oscar Hammerstein from the Broadway play *The King and I*. Copy-
right 1951 by Richard Rodgers & Oscar Hammerstein. Williamson Music,
Inc., owner of publication and allied rights throughout the Western Hem-
isphere and Japan. International copyright secured. ALL RIGHTS RESERVED.
Used by permission.
   Lyrics from Leonard Bernstein's *Mass*. Copyright © 1971 by Leonard
Bernstein and Stephen Schwartz. Used by permission of G. Schirmer, Inc.

ISBN 0-03-062376-6

Acknowledgments

I am indebted to the many wonderful friends and clients whose input and reactions have been invaluable to this book. To all the officers and members of the Ogilvy & Mather worldwide family. To Carol Rinzler, Karen Van Westering, Claire Smith, and Leslie Porte, who thought and edited along with me. To the Department of State and their senior officers and ambassadors for the privilege of sharing historical experiences throughout several administrations, both Republican and Democratic, and to each of those Senators, Prime Ministers, and thousands of chairmen, presidents, executives, and TV news people who entrusted a crucial area of their lives to me.

—DOROTHY SARNOFF

To Milton

Have the daring to accept yourself as a bundle of possibilities and undertake the game of making the most of your best.

—HARRY EMERSON FOSDICK

Contents

Introduction: Rehearsing a President

It was early in the summer of 1979.

"This is Gerry Rafshoon," the pleasant voice on the phone said. "I'd like to ask you if you would work with the President."

"What do you think he needs?" I asked.

"Everything," said Mr. Rafshoon. "How much time will you need?"

"Well," I said, "I would not like to do a Band-Aid operation to get him through one speech. I'd like to do the basics with him."

"That's very sensible. Sounds good."

I told Mr. Rafshoon I'd need at least four hours, preferably two hours on two consecutive days, and that I also would want to meet with the President's writers and anybody else who was involved in his speeches.

"You'll like him," he said. "He's very fast. He's brilliant. And one other thing—he doesn't like to waste time. He'll expect to make that time with you pay off. He won't take any flab."

I laughed. "I don't even say, 'How are you?' to my clients. We go right to work."

"He'll love that," said Gerry Rafshoon.

I flew down to Washington on a Friday, the weekend before the President was to deliver a major speech on television—only I didn't know that then. In the Map Room of the White House, I checked out the videotaping equipment I'd requested. Everything looked perfect for the next day.

On Saturday morning I met with two of the President's speechwriters and Susan Clough, the President's efficient and protective secretary. She looked overworked and skeptical. "What does he usually have on the lectern to speak from?" I asked.

"This is how I've taught him to do it," Mrs. Clough answered. She took out a copy of a speech in which every other word was underlined. "This shows him where to emphasize," she said proudly. "I know the President, and I know what he likes."

"Why, you've already started my technique," I said diplomatically. "How would you like to take it one step further?" With that, I handed Mrs. Clough a copy of one of the President's previous speeches, which I'd marked up for phrasing and emphasis.

She turned around in her chair and read. I studied the room. There were pictures of two teenagers who might have been her brother and sister, a skirt with a needle and thread, some books on Eastern religions. The classical music on her record player took some of the tension out of the air.

I showed Mrs. Clough how to type the speech in separated phrases so that it would be ready for my meeting with Mr. Carter. "Now we must put that in the President's notebook," she said.

I looked at the black looseleaf. "Doesn't the rustling when he turns the pages bother him?" I asked.

"No," she answered briskly. "He likes it that way." She paused. "Oh, God," she exclaimed. "I forgot the title page."

"It's only an exercise," I began.

"No, no. It must say, 'The President of the United States,' and then the date. He's used to it that way."

I met Mr. Carter in the Map Room. He entered with Gerry Rafshoon and one of his aides. He was beaming.

"Okay," I said. "We're ready. Good-bye, everybody."

"Yes," said the President. "Everybody out."

"What would you like to accomplish during my time here?" I asked when we were alone.

He leaned back in his chair and smiled. "Well," he drawled, "everybody tells me I'm pretty good."

"Then," I said kiddingly, "I can turn around and go home, right?"

"I never took a course in this, you know," Mr. Carter said.

I handed him an unmarked copy of the speech in the black leather notebook. Mr. Carter delivered it in a choppy fashion, no flowing phrasing and the famous smile was there.

"I think I have something you'll like," I said and showed him the same speech separated into phrases. "Here's the first rule," I said. "Don't stop the breath until you get to margin right. Finish the phrase, finish the phrase, finish the phrase."

We worked on the speech for nearly an hour.

"This is marvelous," he said.

"One thing to try to get rid of," I said, "is shifting on your feet every time you shift phrases." I suggested he keep his body firm, weight evenly distributed on the balls of both feet, ribcage erect.

"Nobody ever told me that," he said.

"And try to go down in pitch at the ends of phrases and when you want to emphasize."

"They told me to go up to emphasize," said President Carter.

"I don't know who 'they' is," I said, turning on the videotape machine for his next run-through, "but down in pitch will work much better for you."

We watched the playback of his speech. I pointed out to him that the camera exaggerated his warm smile into a grin, and that—grin or smile—it often seemed inappropriate.

"Some day I'd like to deliver a speech that gives me something to smile about," he said ruefully.

The following day, I was struck by the inhumanly hectic pace of the President's schedule, the rushing from one appointment to another. When could he, or any President, have time to think, to mull things over?

We worked for about two hours. Much of that time was devoted to looking over a new speech. It concerned the crisis in Cuba, and Mr. Carter planned to deliver the talk on Monday night. I showed the President how to shorten the overlong sentences, and why they were not spoken sentences. "Could you please come to Camp

David tomorrow so that we can work on it some more?" he asked me.

"Of course," I said.

The next morning, I was driven to Camp David. Susan Clough was the other passenger. She had brought along an enormous hooked rug that she worked on during the ride. "It's my therapy," she said, taking up her latch hook.

When we arrived at the main lodge, I was taken to the dining room. At the end of the long table, the President's appointments secretaries were juggling calendars. I chatted with another man at the table, the President's helicopter pilot. For dessert, he ordered a banana split, astonishing in the company of all those joggers and dieters. "I can't drink when I fly," he explained. "This is my drink."

I met with President Carter in his office. He handed me the new draft of his Cuba speech. He had worked on it all night; it was considerably improved, but it also was considerably changed. We went over it together.

"We need a closing on this," I said. "It just fades away. By the way, you really should have a collection of quotes and anecdotes you can draw on."

"We really should," said the President appreciatively.

"And the word 'important,'" I said, "it's used at least six times in this talk. Do you have a thesaurus here at Camp David?"

"Susan," he called, "call Rosalynn and get the thesaurus." When the book arrived, he read to me from it. "'Crucial'? 'Critical'?" He was an eager student; he had a huge appetite for improvement.

It was getting late. I told President Carter that my husband was expecting me back in Washington. There were several Presidents in my future, I said lightly, but I wanted to keep one husband. President Carter asked Susan to get Milton on the phone. "Milton," he said when my husband answered, "this is Jimmy Carter. Do you mind if I keep your wife a little longer?"

"I've had her for twenty-two years," Milton replied with his characteristic good humor. "I guess I can spare her for an hour or two more."

On Monday afternoon I was back at the White House. I worked with the people who were preparing the Teleprompter roll. The trick is to synchronize the Teleprompter with the notes the speaker has in front of him. That was nicely under control when the President walked in with what amounted to a whole new speech. It was a better speech, but then, as one by one members of the President's staff added their revisions, it became another speech by committee.

It reminded me of Charles Lindbergh's remark when he stepped out of his plane at Le Bourget after his solo transatlantic flight: "It was easy," he said. "I did it alone."

There was hardly time for two run-throughs. The TV staff had to race to put together a new Teleprompter script while the President and I started rehearsing. When the script finally arrived, it did not match the President's.

Despite all the confusion, the President worked like a beaver and never lost his temper, nor his warmth nor his sense of humor.

That night in the Oval Office the President delivered his speech to the world, putting into practice many of the principles on which we had worked. President Carter never did develop into a Franklin Delano Roosevelt or a Winston Churchill, but the speaker who delivered the Presidential State of the Union message in 1980 had come a long way from the speaker of 1976.

Speaking and communicating skills should be sharpened before you sit in the big leather chair, behind the big executive desk, in the big executive office. Once you get there, the demands of public and corporate life are so consuming, that there's little time to develop those needed skills.

All through history, people have been more quickly perceived and accepted as leaders if they could speak persuasively. In these early days of President Reagan's administration, the superb quality of his speechmaking, refined through the years before he took office, has had tremendous impact on the nation.

—DOROTHY SARNOFF

May 1981

1

Finding the Best of Yourself

Presence Is Power
Self-perception vs. Self-deception

Even if what you have to communicate doesn't have quite the earthshaking importance of a President's pronouncements, your ability to communicate effectively and to present the best of yourself and your ideas to others is no less important to you. Be thankful you're not subject to the constant onslaughts of daily events, crises, campaigns, and commitments that are a President's lot. No matter how overburdened your life is, next to a President's, you're on a picnic. If you have the will, you can make the time. And if you take the time, it's easy to learn how to communicate better.

There is a moment in Leonard Bernstein's *Mass* that encapsulates much of what has brought so many people lacking in confidence, forcefulness, and 'presence to work with me and my video camera. The section begins with a solo voice crying out and builds to a frenzied choral lament:

> What I say, I don't feel
> What I feel, I don't say
> I don't know where to start
> How far I can go.
> What I show isn't real

I don't know, I don't know.
What I have, I don't want
What I want, I don't have
What I mean, I don't say.

I have spent more than seventeen years as a communications consultant and "image maker" showing people how to make simple adjustments in their behavior that increased their value to themselves and to others. Those changes literally changed their lives. The people I've worked with learned not merely to communicate, but to communicate with warmth. They changed their attitude toward themselves and toward others, and they changed others' attitudes toward them. Most of these people made such strides in a total of six hours. Many did it in four. So you see, it really must be quite easy.

My clients have ranged from corporation chairpersons who wanted to be more forceful to shy secretaries who lisped. A sales manager, seeing his new self-confident self on videotape, exclaimed, "If I'd done this ten years ago, I wouldn't have had to join Alcoholics Anonymous five years ago." A numbed widow, exploited by her late husband's lawyers, learned more than how to control her adversaries; not long afterward, she was delighting audiences on the lecture circuit.

There is an old and charming story about a little girl who visited a sculptor one day as he started work on a fresh block of marble. Some weeks later, the child visited the sculptor again. Under his hands, a lion was taking shape from the stone. Astonished, the little girl tilted her head to one side and asked, "Did you know all the time that there was a lion inside?"

I've often thought that the closed-circuit television I work with is what a chisel is to marble. I recently prepared an author for a series of television appearances. She marveled at the instant change in her own appearance and in that of other authors I had taped. She couldn't believe the "before" and "after" shots were of the same people, taken one day apart. I told her that my father had been a plastic surgeon, and that when he changed people's appearance, their behavior changed. I change people's behavior and their appearance changes.

I start with a single premise: There is a better self inside every one of us. The question is, how to find it. You are unique, but there may be a variety of yous inside you. This book will help you to select the best of your selves, to redesign your behavior and come out with a better you.

If there is a secret to the success I have had in helping people improve their lives, it is that I accept no one who is not strongly motivated. The ability to present yourself and your ideas well is to your skills and your personality as sunshine is to a stained-glass window. The optimistic promise of this book is that if you are willing to contribute some effort, by the time you have read the last page, you will be saying more of what you mean, and having more of what you want.

PRESENCE IS POWER

"Not everything that is faced can be changed, but nothing can be changed until it is faced," said Franklin Delano Roosevelt. Redesigning yourself begins with sharpening your perceptions—of others and of yourself. Try to split-screen your mind and see on one side the public figures and personal acquaintances who have commanded and held your attention as they spoke and on the other side those people who turned you off, who made you want to go to sleep or run away.

Very probably, Helmut Schmidt, Anne Armstrong, John F. Kennedy, and Barbara Jordan will be on the positive side; Bobby Kennedy and Richard Nixon may be among those on the negative. Think about the differences between the two groups. Contrast Richard Nixon with Jack Kennedy.

Consider the two men's eyes. Jack Kennedy had "talking eyes." When he looked at you, even through a television camera, he seemed to be looking directly at you; his eyes sparkled, expressed warmth, sincerity, credibility. (Whether or not President Kennedy actually felt warm and sincere or just seemed to is not the point. I've worked with enough politicians to know that good "seeming-to-be" is what counts.) Nixon's eyes were another story. Right before my first consultation with the State Department, I called them and said, "I think you'd better know that *Esquire* magazine is coming out with an article about my work. And in it I say that ex-President Nixon has eyes as dull as two blueberries. Can I still come?" They said, "Rush!"

Try to recall President Kennedy's face as he spoke. Like most of those who hold our attention, his face was alive and animated. Robert Kennedy had the same New England accent as his brother and was nearly as articulate, but he was a speed talker, and he invariably inflected up at the ends of sentences. The expression on his face rarely changed. Robert Kennedy was monofaced, monotoned, and monopaced.

If you identify the qualities of speakers who have captured your attention, you will come up with a list something like this:

> Confidence and ease (which makes you
>   feel at ease with them)
> Authority
> Conviction
> Credibility
> Sincerity
> Warmth
> Animation
> Enthusiasm
> Vitality
> Intensity
> Concern (they seem to be personally
>   involved with your involvement)
> Empathy
> Eye contact
> Conversational tone
> Variety of pitch, pacing, projection, and phrasing

All of those qualities add up to one word—presence. Those who have presence command our attention; they know how to project the best of themselves. They exert a profound influence on others. A room lights up because they're in it.

SELF-PERCEPTION VS. SELF-DECEPTION

Once you've identified the positive qualities in others, it's time to examine yourself. Divide a sheet of paper into three columns. In the first column, list your positive qualities. If you're like almost every client I've worked with, you'll go blank after five or six. Even people with outstanding achievements do so after listing a few modest adjectives. (If I'd asked you to begin by listing your flaws, you would have had no problems.) To get started, consider the adjectives that follow. Write down the ones that fit you. You'll probably end up with a list of twenty or thirty.

TURN-ON QUALITIES

accommodating
accurate
active
adroit
adventurous
affable
agreeable
alert
amiable
analytical
appealing
artistic
assertive

balanced
beautiful
believable
benevolent
bold
brainy
brave
bright
brilliant
businesslike

calm
candid
capable
captivating
careful
charitable
charming
cheerful
chic
clear
colorful

comfortable
compassionate
complimentary
concentrated
considerable
consoling
cooperative
courteous
creative
credible
cultured
curious

dapper
dashing
decent
decisive
dedicated
definite
delightful
dependable
descriptive
desirable
determined
devout
diplomatic
discerning
discreet
distinctive
distinguished
durable
dynamic

eager
earnest
ebullient

economical
educated
efficient
eloquent
empathetic
enduring
energetic
enterprising
entertaining
enthusiastic
erudite
explicit
expressive

fair-minded
faithful
firm
fit
flexible
fond
forceful
forgiving
frank
friendly
funny

gallant
generous
genial
gentle
gifted
go-getting
gracious
grateful
gutsy

handsome

handy

happy

hardheaded

hardy

healthy

helpful

honorable

hopeful

hospitable

humane

humorous

idealistic

imaginative

impartial

important

impressive

incisive

individualistic

industrious

informative

informed

ingenious

innovative

insightful

intelligent

intense

interesting

intuitive

inventive

involved

jolly

joyful

judicious

just

knowledgeable

learned

level-headed

lighthearted

likable

lionhearted

lively

logical

lovable

loving

loyal

magnanimous

magnetic

masterful

merciful

methodical

moderate

modest

moral

motivated

musical

natural

neat

nervy

nice

nonchalant

nonconforming

objective

obliging

observant

offbeat

open-minded

optimistic

orderly

original

outgoing

pace-setting

passionate

patient

patriotic

peaceable

penetrating

perceptive

perspicacious

persuasive

pleasant

plucky

poised

popular

principled

productive

professional

proficient

prudent

purposeful

questioning

quick-witted

quotable

radiant

rational

ready

realistic

reasonable

receptive

refreshing

relaxed

reliable

resilient

responsible

rigorous
rugged

scholarly
self-assured
self-confident
self-controlled
self-sacrificing
sensible
sensitive
sentimental
sharp
sincere
skilled
smart
sociable
spirited
spontaneous
spunky
strong
studious
stylish
successful

tactful
take-charge

tasteful
temperate
tenacious
tender
thorough
thoughtful
tolerant
tractable
tranquil
true
trusting
trustworthy

unbiased
uncomplaining
understanding
unflinching
unpretentious
unusual
upright
upstanding
urbane
useful

valiant
valuable

varied
venerable
venturesome
veracious
versatile
vigilant
vigorous
virtuous
vital

warm
watchful
well-adjusted
well-balanced
well-behaved
well-informed
whimsical
wholesome
winning
wise
witty
worldly

youthful

zealous
zestful

Most of us have very little awareness of how we come across to others. Seeing and hearing ourselves on videotape is the quickest way to perceive ourselves as others perceive us. The vice-president of a large can company came to see me because his wife, who had been watching him put audiences to sleep for years, gave him the course as a Christmas present. Martin's reaction, when he saw himself on playback was, "My Lord, I look like a funeral director. I should be selling coffins, not beer cans." In three two-hour sessions, we recycled Martin from dull, drab, and diffident to convincing, compelling, and charismatic.

But even without a video camera, you can begin analyzing yourself. Once you've acknowledged your positive qualities, list in the second column what you consider to be your defects and flaws—qualities about yourself that you'd like to remove or change. Recall others' reactions to you, or ask someone whose opinion you trust. Try to be objective as well as subjective. List in the third column what you think you're missing that you'd like to add.

Now that you have your lists, you're ready to begin. In the next chapter, you're going to learn about the components that make up presence. Next, you'll go step by step through writing, preparing, and delivering a talk or presentation. You'll learn not only how to deliver a talk better than you ever thought you could; you'll also learn how to apply individual parts of the formula for the control of nervousness, which will give you self-confidence in any stress-provoking situation. In the final section of the book, you'll learn how you can communicate presence in every aspect of your daily life and make the most of your best every minute of the day.

2

Putting Your Best You Forward

Tone Talk
Eye Talk
Face Talk
Body Talk
Appearance and Clothes Talk

Coopers & Lybrand, the nation's third-largest accounting firm, has two new categories in its "Confidential Performance Report":

EXECUTIVE PRESENCE

Initial impression created (self-confidence, poise, tact, maturity, appearance)

Lasting impression created (gains the professional respect and confidence of others)

General business knowledge

COMMUNICATION

Speaking (clarity, ease, conciseness)

Writing (clarity, conciseness, organization)

Listening (attentiveness, responsiveness, understanding)

So far as I know, Coopers & Lybrand is the first firm to set down those qualities in black and white (and to rate its employees on them from Outstanding to Unsatisfactory), but every firm—and every person you meet—makes those value judgments.

How are you judged? Everything about you speaks—not just the words you choose to express your thoughts. You have five message givers: the tone of your voice, your eyes, your face, your bearing, your dress.

Separately and together, all of those message givers should project ease, concern, authority, and confidence—those qualities that make up presence and enhance your self-presentation.

TONE TALK

The Wall Street Journal ran a story recently about a speech expert who claimed to improve a person's voice in only six months. Our techniques can improve a voice in six hours. The wife of a very famous singer flew in from California with a problem—her voice irritated her husband. His sensitive ear found her high-pitched tone abrasive. Two two-hour sessions later, she flew back to the Coast with a voice that was as soothing as a cello.

A quick flip through this chapter will show you that there are about as many pages devoted to tone of voice as there are to all the other message givers combined. That's because there are so many different ways your tone of voice can be improved, thereby improving your presence.

Tone alone can send a message, as you know if you've ever heard Richard Burton reading the phone book. Consider the change in meaning that a change in tone can bring. Say, "Please come here," first seductively, then angrily. The words don't change, but the message does. I received the best reviews of my stage career in a part that had the worst lines. When I complained about the dreadful writing to my coach, she reminded me that when I sang opera in a foreign language I had to convey much of the character's feeling through tone, not words. She suggested I do the same for the ridiculous dialogue and work for meaning through tone alone. I had the audience sobbing; Brooks Atkinson called the performance "brilliant."

Tone influences us so greatly because our bodies are sound sensitive. A shrill voice produces the same involuntary muscle tightening and constriction of blood vessels in its hearer that a jackhammer in the street or chalk screeching on a blackboard does. A strident, abrasive voice causes irritation and the wish to escape from the source of the sound. A thin, whispery voice is tiring because you have to strain to hear it. An uninflected drone has the effect of a sleeping pill. Sound can cause emotional reactions; the physical effect of a voice can make a listener buy or resist, become a believer or a nonbeliever.

I divide listeners into three types. The first are those who listen only for content; they respond strongly to an Adlai Stevenson, are fascinated by the polysyllabic exhalations of a William F. Buckley. The second group responds almost entirely to the sound—to the cadence, momentum, and rhythm of a speaker like Martin Luther King or Billy Graham. But by far the largest number of people are affected by both content and delivery. Of all speakers in recent memory, Winston Churchill and Franklin Roosevelt had the best combined appeal.

Very often, as Marshall McLuhan put it, the medium is the message; your medium is your presentation of yourself and your voice is an important element of that self-presentation. Don't let it be a negative factor. To find out, you really need a tape recorder. A mirror can tell you something about the visual you—whether you're using your hands too much, for instance, or talking without moving your lips or eyes. But the best mirror for the voice is a tape recorder. Since a self-conscious tone may creep into your voice if you record it just for appraisal, put the tape recorder next to your telephone and record yourself occasionally during calls. When you have several conversations taped, listen to the playback.

If you think your voice has a specific defect—lisping, for example, or shrillness—see the Appendix for diagnoses and suggestions. In this section, we're going to show you how to improve the tone of your voice and consequently add color to your message through the variety of the four P's—Projection, Pitch, Phrasing, and Pacing.

Projection

You can make your voice say "vigorous" when you're tired, "young" when you're over seventy. Watch out if your voice says "fatigued" when you feel fresh, "weak" when you're strong, "frustrated" when you're fulfilled. If your voice lacks vitality, vigor, enthusiasm, intensity, that's because you are not energizing it, not supporting your voice with the pressure of your breath.

What does that mean? Picture a Ping-Pong ball bobbing on the crest of a fountain. It stays up there because the pressure of the water is maintained. Imagine that the ball is your voice and the fountain is the force of your breath. If the pressure of the water remains constant, the Ping-Pong ball will stay up there. But if the pressure is decreased, the ball drops.

It takes no great energy to support the voice. The breath needed to utter a word amounts to less than one fiftieth of one millionth of one horsepower. If all the people on Earth were to say the same sentence at the same time ("Things are tough all over," is one possibility), the total energy created by their collective breath would be too trifling to run a car across an intersection. Breath control is not a matter of how much air you take in but of how you support the air or give it pressure on the way out. A sip of air is all you need to take in to speak a long sentence.

The first step toward achieving a vital tone is Executive Posture —chest up, stomach tucked in. The second step is learning how to use the muscles that support your voice to make it project authority and energy. Have you ever noticed that when you speak emotionally—in anger, outrage, defiance, command—the support muscles in your midriff work harder? They're in the act of contracting.

Sit on the edge of a straight-backed chair, chest up, head high. With both hands, run your fingers down the middle of your chest until you feel muscle. Now run the fingers of each hand along the sides of your ribcage as it splays. These are the sides of what I call the Vital Triangle; the base is the straight line across the widest separation of ribs; it's about three inches above your waist or belt line. Trace the outline of the triangle to familiarize yourself with it.

There are two ways to feel how your support muscles should be working when you speak. Sitting erect on your chair, put the palm of your hand over the triangle area. Stand up and sit down quickly four or five times. (DO NOT DO THIS IF YOU HAVE A HEART CONDITION.) Observe that as you pull yourself to a standing position, the muscles under your hand contract, then pull back and tighten toward the spine. As you sit down, they relax.

Now stand and face a wall, a bit less than an arm's length away. Put one foot in front of the other in a lunging position. Now put both hands on the wall at shoulder height and try to push that wall down on a slow count of four. You should feel your vital triangle muscles tightening and contracting back toward your spine.

Even when you're speaking quietly, the muscles of your vital triangle should be in this contracting action. A lot of voice strain nowadays comes from trying to talk over deafening disco decibels. But even in a crowded, noisy room you can project your voice above the hubbub without strain by constantly contracting those vital triangle muscles and sending the breath up to your vocal cords with pressure.

The following exercises will show you how your support muscles can work so that you project easily, with no voice strain.

1. The Teakettle. Inhale quickly, taking a normal small sip of air, not a big breath. Big breaths make you tense. By a sip of air, I mean a little gasp—enough to smell a flower, but through your mouth. Exhale, very slowly, a small stream of air with a hiss through your lower teeth. As you exhale, slowly contract your vital triangle muscles. Prolong the contraction or exhalation for as long as you can. Pull those muscles back as you would pull back oars when rowing a boat. Pull B-A-C-K, pull B-A-C-K, pull B-A-C-K. Count to forty silently on each pullback. Then try for fifty, then for sixty. Continue to do the contraction combined with the teakettle hissing until you can count silently to about 130.

2. The Flickering Flame. Remember the scene in *My Fair Lady* where Professor Higgins shows Eliza how to blow a thin stream of air at a candle so that it flickers but never goes out? Pretend that your index finger is a candle. Hold it about ten inches from your face and direct your breath at it gently in a thin stream, keeping your mouth in a blowing position. If you're uncertain about whether your breath is touching your finger, wet your finger, and the evaporation of the moisture will signal the passing air. As you exhale, monitor your vital triangle with your other hand and feel the contraction. This is how your vital triangle should feel when you speak on the telephone or to someone less than ten feet away.

Next, extend your arm and aim the stream of air at your finger. You'll find the muscle tension becomes even stronger, the support gets into muscles lower down. The farther off your finger is, the deeper the support must go to project your breath. To blow the candle out at arm's length, you use muscles in your groin, your thighs, your buttocks, behind your knees, perhaps even at the back of your calves and down to your ankles. They are all backing up the vital triangle control muscles to provide that extra support and projection.

3. The Projection Punch. This exercise has been the greatest voice-giver to clients. Say each of the words below three times on one breath—quietly for the lower-case version, at medium volume for the first repetition, emphatically for the second repetition. The lower-case words should be spoken as if to someone ten feet away; the capitalized words as if to someone at distances of ten and twenty-five feet. Pretend you're on a balcony projecting down to the other end of the room. That will help you resist the temptation to raise the pitch of your voice. Each time you say a word, s-t-r-e-t-c-h the vowel or diphthong. Make fists and punch out, arm's length, as you say each word; punch harder and farther the second and third times. Make your vital triangle muscles imitate the tension in your punching fists.

so	SO	SO!
toe	TOE	TOE!
no	NO	NO!
dough	DOUGH	DOUGH!
foe	FOE	FOE!
la	LA	LA!
baa	BAA	BAA!
fah	FAH	FAH!
ma	MA	MA!
pa	PA	PA!
rah	RAH	RAH!
ta	TA	TA!
push	PUSH	PUSH!
pull	PULL	PULL!
rush	RUSH	RUSH!
buy	BUY	BUY!
cry	CRY	CRY!
die	DIE	DIE!
high	HIGH	HIGH!
lie	LIE	LIE!
my	MY	MY!
tie	TIE	TIE!

Pitch

An airline once asked me to help one of its stewardesses, a candidate in a beauty contest; she inflected up at the end of every sentence and sounded like a cat yowling on a back fence. A few lessons got her inflecting down, and the lower pitch gave her a velvet voice that matched her beauty.

When you want someone to relax or to feel safe with you, when you talk to an infant, when you speak to someone you love, you probably lower the pitch of your voice. A little-girl voice is inappropriate in a woman who holds a position of importance; men with high voices lack authority. A lower register enhances almost everyone's image.

To find out how low your potential pitch is, place your hand flat on your chest right under your collarbone and say "low," three times, going down in pitch each time, as if you were walking down steps. Put your palm on your chest bone and request vibrations there as your voice descends. (You can use the words in the "projection punch" exercise to do this, making your voice go low, lower, lowest as you go from column to column.) Aim for the lowest pitch at which you can speak comfortably. To help find a lower voice and chest resonance, try the following:

Sit in a chair and place your feet squarely on the floor, about twelve inches apart. Open this book to the Projection Punch drill and put it on the floor between your heels. Bend over from your waist toward the book, your head dangling, your arms hanging loose. Your fingers should be like limp tassels touching the floor. Relax completely. Now begin reading from the book, contracting the muscles of your vital triangle as you do so. Your voice should resonate in your chest, and your pitch should be lower in this position. Listen to this sound and feel the sensation of it in your body; this is the sound you want. Then straighten up, trying to retain the voice quality and sensation of resonance in the chest that you had in the dangling position. (For additional exercises on lowering pitch, see Appendix.)

Raising the pitch or inflecting up at the ends of sentences makes you sound singsong and transmits tentativeness, lack of assurance, and sometimes even incompetence. To sound more assertive, go down in pitch at the ends of sentences, phrases, or words preceding commas, and on any word or phrase you wish to emphasize.

1. Say these two sentences in your normal way: "The desire for quality in business can be contagious. Let's start an epidemic." Now say them going down in pitch at the end of each phrase. If you tape the two versions, you'll note the sound of authority in the down-pitched one.

2. Go down in pitch at the end of a question. Say, "Can we have faith in our leaders?" inflecting up on the final word. Now go down in pitch on the final word. Try saying a more ordinary sentence: "How long are we going to wait?" both ways. Lowering your voice on the final word makes you sound more assertive.

Phrasing

If your speech is choppy or staccato it will sound like Morse Code. Your speech should have the smooth flow of a bowed cello, not the short hiccough blips of a piccolo. Try the following for more flowing phrasing.

Read aloud, making one word lead, almost ooze, into the next:

1. May the sun shine warm upon your face,
   And the rain fall soft upon your fields,
   And until we meet again,
   May God hold you in the palm of His hand.

2. To every thing there is a season, and a time to every purpose under the heaven:
   A time to be born, and a time to die;
   A time to plant, and a time to pluck up that which is planted;
   A time to kill, and a time to heal;
   A time to break down, and a time to build up;
   A time to weep, and a time to laugh;
   A time to mourn, and a time to dance;
   A time to cast away stones, and a time to gather stones together;
   A time to embrace, and a time to refrain from embracing;
   A time to get, and a time to lose;
   A time to keep, and a time to cast away;
   A time to rend, and a time to sew;
   A time to keep silence, and a time to speak;
   A time to love, and a time to hate;
   A time of war, and a time of peace.

—ECCLESIASTES 3:1–8

Declarations, exhortations, accusations, threats, warnings—all are potential candidates for what I call lay-out phrases. By stretching out the words, and giving energy to the phrase, you emphasize the meaning. Imagine that you have a piece of elastic three inches long and three inches wide. Hold it between your hands and puuullll it until it stretches to double its length. That's the tension and energy you want in speaking a lay-out phrase.

Read the sentences below, putting that tension into each italicized phrase. Don't pause until you get to the end of a phrase. Instruct yourself to finish the phrase, finish the phrase, finish the phrase.

> It's time to choose between *changing-the-earth* and *preserving-some-of-it-as-it-is.* Converting natural resources into money *poses-a-threat-to-human-well-being.* It is time to *stop-the-golding-of-the-earth* and *encourage-the-greening-of-the-earth.*
>
> —RUSSELL PETERSON

> We ought to engage in pursuits which are *loving-not-maligning; constructive-not-destructive, orderly-not-chaotic.* Then we may feel that we have the right to *a-great-joy* and *a-great-peace.*
>
> —MALCOLM MUGGERIDGE

Pacing

Hubert Humphrey, said Barry Goldwater, talked so fast that listening to him was like trying to read *Playboy* with your wife turning the pages. President Johnson used to dawdle so, that a new international crisis could have exploded before he finished briefing the country on the current one. Although there are considerable variations in regional speaking patterns, the ideal rate of speech for the English language in America is about 170 words per minute. The rate should not be constant, of course—you want variety of pacing, not monotony. Moreover, the pacing of speech varies, in business and in social life, faster on Monday morning than on Friday afternoon, different depending on whether you're at lunch or dinner, in a face-to-face encounter or on the telephone. You should speak faster on radio than on television and faster on television than you do in an office or living room. But despite those variations, a person who normally speaks at 180 words per minute or more sounds perilously close to a machine gun rat-a-tat-tat and irritates his listeners. Conversely, talking too slowly, less than 150 words per minute, is likely to bore.

Read aloud from the beginning of this section. Stop at the end of one minute and mark the last word you spoke. If you didn't reach the phrase "machine gun rat-a-tat-tat" in sixty seconds, you were reading too slowly. If you got too far past the beginning of this paragraph, you were beginning to sound like that machine gun.

The faster you speak, the more you sacrifice color, intensity, and flow. If you're a speed talker, try this:

Using the second hand of a watch or clock, count from one to ten, first in five seconds, then in ten, then in twenty. You'll gradually slow yourself down.

Varying pitch, pacing, phrasing, and projection adds color and variety to your speech; they give cadence, or melody, to your spoken phrases. When you color your speech with those four P's, you can create almost as many combinations with a single sentence as there are in a hand of seven-card stud.

EYE TALK

"People can't understand each other if they don't look at each other," says Barbara Walters. "I look straight into the camera hoping that by my eye contact I'll be able to reach people in the most personal way." Speaking without making eye contact is like talking with a bag over your head. Eyes convey the messages of approval, love, interest, sincerity, credibility, enthusiasm, excitement—and all of the negative emotions as well.

Warren Christopher, who as Deputy Secretary of State was so tireless and admirable as the chief American negotiator during the Iranian hostage crisis, often consulted with me before his appearances on "Meet the Press" and "Face the Nation." Working with Deputy Secretary Christopher was a privilege. He adopted every discipline I suggested and instantly put it into practice. Every time I left him he graciously said, "Dorothy, you give me so much confidence." I wonder if he ever realized how much the gift of his graciousness has meant to me.

I started working with Mr. Christopher shortly after he returned from a trip to Taiwan, where his car had been pelted with rocks and rotten tomatoes. The incident had been widely reported in the newspapers and on TV. He said to me jokingly, "I had hoped to go down in history for something more than being a mark for rotten vegetables." Watching him on TV as he greeted the hostages that historic night in Algeria, there could be no doubt in anyone's mind that he had made his mark in history brilliantly, modestly, indelibly. I loved what Dan Rather said, "He worked so hard, for so long, for so many."

The Deputy Secretary is a brilliant, modest, nonaggressive man. We discovered, as we role-played interviews, that he tended to look a little too self-effacing, with eyes either cast down or over-blinking. This robbed him of impact. We overcame that by having him "eye-sweep" from one person to another as he spoke, not blinking until the end of each phrase. Now his look had an impact that matched his impact as a diplomat.

Eyes can project confidence and inspire instant trust. Think of the unspoken messages you've sent and received. A woman at a party can know that a man she's never met before would like to see her home simply by decoding the language of his eyes from across the room.

I've been on most of the talk shows, and the best host by far was David Frost—his eyes talked for twenty-eight minutes. They seemed to dance with joy as he listened to his guests, signaling to the most uninspiring among them, "Fabulous!" "Fascinating!" "Interesting!" And the guest became fabulous. To be a good lis-tener, your eyes should say, "I am listening," and convey empathy and concern. When you're the talker, watch your listeners' eyes to see whether or not you're holding their interest and attention. Keep a mirror by your telephone for a few days. Each time you have a conversation, check to see whether your eyes are talking and say-ing what your words are.

The more neurotic a person, the more brief his gaze. (Schizo-phrenics and depressives have very short looking times; autistic children have the shortest looking time of all.) There is something disconcerting and not at all confidence-inspiring about a person who has to retreat from your eyes into his thinking office, search-ing the ceiling or walls or the floor or his hands for the next thought. Try to be eye-to-eye 90 percent of the time.

When I say eye-to-eye, I don't mean stare—that makes people uncomfortable. You may not have noticed that it's not possible to look directly into both eyes at once (try it). You usually focus on the person's stronger eye. What you're after instead is a gently moving gaze. Speaking to a person to one eye, moving occasionally to the other, gives action to your face. When you're speaking to more than one person, make sure you give everyone the benefit of your eye contact, by "eye-sweeping."

FACE TALK

"Energy is beauty," said designer Elsa Peretti. "A Ferrari with an empty tank doesn't run." A noncommunicating face has no energy; it's as off-putting as absent eyes. A nonexpressive face doesn't put others at ease; the other person wonders, "Doesn't he like me?" "Is he uncomfortable?" Humanity is hidden.

The stone face is characteristic of many cultures—the inscrutable Oriental, the proverbially stiff-upper-lipped Englishman are two stereotypes, and we Americans have our share of Henry Kissingers. Researchers have discovered remarkable regional variations in this country. Southerners smile more often, and New Englanders smile less, but, says Professor Ray L. Birdwhistell, the Southerner's smile may be a way of reducing aggression and the New Englander's reserve doesn't show unfriendliness so much as it does a reluctance to engage in an inappropriately personal relationship. (Think of the face of the person in the seat next to you on the plane who doesn't want to talk.) As for New Yorkers, their "mask of nonparticipation" is so fixed that when a New Yorker outside of New York smiles a great deal, people think he's a salesman.

Animation is the greatest cosmetic there is—and by animation I don't mean smiling, I mean aliveness. "Some of us are not great beauties," said Helen Gurley Brown, the editor of *Cosmopolitan.* "That notion is responsible for whatever success I've had in life, because not being beautiful, I had to make up for it with brains, charm, drive, and personality."

An animated face is a beautiful face. I once asked a famous bachelor what attracted him in a woman's face. "I don't look for a pretty face," he replied, "I look for a happy face." Animation boosts your personality, gives you a glow that casts a becoming light on others and puts them at ease with you.

I've worked with diplomats who felt they needed a somber,

unreadable face until I pointed out to them that an animated face can be noncommittal too. Women who don't move their facial muscles for fear of getting wrinkles don't realize that a sagging face without animation looks ten years older than a face with its muscles lifted. One woman who kept her face frozen because she thought a large scar on her cheek would be less noticeable that way saw in playback on my TV monitor that when her face was animated one didn't focus on the scar. Walking around with a droopy face is like letting your stockings or socks fall down around your ankles.

Again, the mirror by your telephone. Is your face saying what your words are, or is, "That's wonderful news!" accompanied by an indifferent, cold face? If people ask you what the matter is when everything is fine, put animation into your face. That doesn't mean have a plastic, phony, politican's smile, but rather an expression of vitality and participation. Beverly Sills once made a fine distinction. "I'm cheerful," Miss Sills said, "I'm not happy, but I'm cheerful. There's a big difference. A happy person has no cares at all; a cheerful person has cares but learns to ignore them."

To learn about animating your face, try this:

1. Look into a mirror and run your face through the gamut of emotions—sympathy, doubt, cheerfulness, dread, worry, rage, astonishment, panic, delight, love, ecstasy. The more pleasant and positive the feeling, the more flattering to your face.

2. Lift up your cheeks so that they make "love apples" right under your eyes. Looking at yourself in the mirror, think of the most pleasant experience you've had all month. Watch your face light up. Now dim the light some, as if you were remembering the next most pleasant experience. Notice that the upper parts of your cheeks still are slightly elevated. That's the expression to strive for when you want others to perceive you as warm, responsive, and alive.

BODY TALK

The recently appointed head of personnel of a Fortune-500 company consulted me because she felt she wasn't being taken seriously by her male colleagues. "I have an M.B.A. from Harvard," she said, "but in meetings, they just ignore me." It was easy to see that Marian's problems began the moment she entered a room: her body sagged. It said "passive," not "active." When she sat down, she looked like a rumpled sleeping bag.

Good carriage made Marian another woman. With her head high and her shoulders straight, her whole personality was more commanding; she had changed her image. "The kind of people we want," said Marian's boss when he promoted her a year later to vice-president, "are the kind we can put up front. Those are the ones we want to advance, the ones who'll get to the top."

When a good actor walks on stage, what does he have that commands attention even before he speaks? What he has is presence—presence communicated by body intensity. Body intensity or body tension (not tenseness) is created by contracting the muscles of your body exactly as you do when you serve at tennis or drive off a tee in golf. If all your muscles are in contraction when you're sitting or standing, you will have body intensity and presence. That doesn't mean holding yourself in military-stiff posture. It means stretching tall. Maybe you can understand it this way: again take hold of a rubber band; feel it slack; then stretch it as far as it will go without breaking. That should give you an idea of the degree of tension you should feel in all of your muscles when you want your body to say: Authority.

Of all the message givers, bearing is the one that instantly communicates presence. Look at yourself right now. Are you slumping in your chair, chest sunk in? Look down at your waist—is there a spare tire? Bad posture does more than make you look older and less attractive. It negatively alters others' perceptions of you. You diminish yourself every time you walk into a room if you slouch on your feet or sit slumped in a chair. The message you're sending with your bearing is, "So what?"

Positive posture—I call it Executive Posture—gives you the look of authority. Standing or sitting, your head and chin up, ribcage high, stomach tucked in, equals body intensity. To understand what I mean by positive posture, try the following:

1. Stand up, pushing your head against an imaginary ceiling until you feel the stretch. Push your shoulders down as if you were carrying two heavy suitcases. Your weight should be evenly distributed on the balls of both feet.

2. Sitting in a chair, make believe you're a puppet with a string attached to the top of your head. Tighten the string, pulling yourself up tall. Incline your torso slightly forward.

To give yourself an air of authority in a meeting or while talking to another person, choose a straight-backed chair. Sit chest up, torso inclined slightly forward. Only the lower part of your spine should lean against the back of the chair. Always remember: air between you and the back of the chair from your waist up.

Use that posture even when you're listening. One insurance company counseled its salesmen to "sit back and listen." Wrong. Sitting back makes you look passive, robs you of body intensity. If you hold your upper torso in contraction and incline slightly forward, you inject yourself actively into the scene. You look interested.

You'll discover that executive posture reduces fatigue. That's because your head weighs over twenty pounds, and carrying it high on top of your stretching spinal column is easier on your back muscles than letting it sag. You'll feel lighter. Sit in executive posture for a moment and then slump; notice how much heavier your body feels.

By standing and sitting in executive posture, your bearing will project confidence and authority. You won't look intimidated; you'll look in control—and you will have presence.

As much as body intensity can contribute to presence, nervous mannerisms can detract from it. By now everybody knows that you talk with your body as well as with your words. Don't let your body say "nervous."

Anthropologist Desmond Morris has researched nonverbal signals of nervousness by studying the behavior of people when they're lying. Morris reports that tone of voice and facial expression are the signals easiest to control; fidgeting is the giveaway (which means, do your lying over the telephone or while your body's involved in a mechanical task like threading a needle or parking a car). In one experiment, student nurses first were asked to tell the truth and then to lie convincingly. When lying, the nurses touched their noses and mouths more frequently.

The worst case of the fidgets I ever ran across was Senator

Daniel Moynihan. We were guest speakers at a convention. During the course of his speech, he scratched his chest until he scratched a hole in his shirt, tossed a lock of hair off his forehead constantly, and peppered his speech with "uh's."

More signals of uneasiness: scratching noses, swinging legs, twirling pens or pencils, picking cuticles, or fiddling with jewelry. One client of mine realized he unwound a box of paper clips every day. The editor of a major women's magazine, who wanted to be more effective in meetings, was blissfully unaware that she twitched her nose like a rabbit whenever she spoke.

As you use the tape recorder to learn about the tone of your voice, you can identify many nervous mannerisms in that mirror by your telephone.

A way to control fidgeting hands instantly is to dig the thumbnail of one hand into the palm of the other. You may get stigmata, but your hands will be nailed together while you talk or sit and listen attentively.

It's easy to rid yourself of other negative mannerisms too. One government official who consulted me worked his jaw every time he had to field a difficult question at a press conference, or whenever reporters teased him about the lady he was seeing. His John Wayne jaw muscles made him look like a man readying for a fight. By keeping his lips slightly parted as he listened to questions, he couldn't grind his jaw. What worked for him was a behavior-modification gimmick that's the best trick I know for curing nervous mannerisms.

The Red Dot Cure: Buy a package of tiny, round, bright-red self-adhering stickers. Put the stickers, suitably inscribed, on your watch, your wallet, your telephone, your desk—wherever you're likely to notice them often. If you want to remind yourself to light up your face, draw a smile face on the stickers; if you'd like to break yourself of saying, "Uh," or "y'know," write the word, crossed out, on the red dots. The constant reminder will help you to modify your behavior quickly.

Stickers are also helpful for people who speak too quickly or too slowly. A diplomat who speed-talked consulted me on the eve of an important television appearance. I had him put a red sticker, marked with the word "SLOW," on the inside seam of his trousers where the sticker would catch his eye when he crossed his legs. His peripheral vision kept him aware of the sticker reminder, and he paced himself neatly.

Incidentally, the red dots also can help you if you're overweight and the culprit is insufficient willpower. Strew the stickers around wherever you'll see them when temptation strikes. And if you are overweight, give some thought to the signals obesity sends before you skip to the next section. William DeJong, a social psychologist who studies physical deviance, has concluded from his experiments that unless fat people have a plausible explanation for their weight, such as a glandular condition, or make it clear that they're on a diet, people tend to assume they are bad, dirty, passive, dull, and weak.

DeJong gave each of 226 high school students photographs of a normal and an obese girl, together with a copy of each girl's answers to a "background information" questionnaire about her weight and health. The answers actually were written by DeJong, who gave the obese girl three different explanations for her excessive weight. A different group of students got each one.

The students, asked to give their first impressions of the girls in the photographs, rated the obese girl as less dynamic than the slender girl, regardless of which explanation was offered for her excess weight. When she had no explanation, she was liked least. If she claimed to be dieting or offered a glandular "excuse," she was liked better—the students thought she had more self-control and found her "sweeter" and "cleaner."

Stigmatizing the character of the obese may be unfair, but that's the way it is.

APPEARANCE AND CLOTHES TALK

In a delightful *New Yorker* cartoon, a dowager with her husband in tow beseeches a clothing salesman: "He's a dignitary. Make him look like one." I can't count the number of times management people have asked me to spruce up a valued employee. For reasons of tact, the employee usually is told he's being sent to me to improve his presentation style or speechmaking skills, but the real objective is improving his appearance. "I can't bring myself to tell him," one boss complained to me, "but he's so badly dressed, I hate to bring him with me to meetings. And he's one of my best men."

The man who turned up was tall and skinny and wore the suit of a fat man; there was room inside for two of him. His pockets bulged with items so heavy they pulled his suit even more out of shape.

For starters, I asked him to show me what he was carrying in his pockets. He cleared a space in front of him and unpacked: two fat wallets, a pack of cigarettes, two matchbooks, a handkerchief rolled into a ball, a package of cough drops, two old airline folders, a fat notebook, a nail file, a keycase, a screwdriver . . .

"A screwdriver?" I asked.

"To fix my glasses when the hinge gets loose," he explained.

. . . a pair of sunglasses in a case, a pair of reading glasses, several letters, and a report folded in half.

"Put it all back and let's videotape you," I told him.

He studied himself in silence. "When I get home tonight," he told me earnestly, "I'm going to burn this suit."

I'm not an expert on dress (although I can take credit for getting Menachem Begin to get rid of his menacing, thick, black-rimmed eyeglasses), but I can mention several things, besides bulging pockets and ill-fitting suits, that detract from a look of authority and send the wrong signals about you. (If you're a "creative type," of course, you were hired to send your own signals and make your own rules. Just skip to the next chapter.)

Eyeglasses are a good place to start. If you wear prescription glasses, the frame should be in proportion to the size and shape of your face. Heavy black frames give you a stark look; frames close to the color of your hair are usually the most flattering.

Avoid Easy-Rider frames or those with a cocker spaniel droop. They make you look mournful. Metal frames make you look like a bookkeeper (not a problem if you are a bookkeeper, or want to look like one). Some opticians now have closed-circuit television on which you can see yourself in a variety of frames. If your optician doesn't yet, bring a quick-print camera with you; it's almost impossible to judge which frames are becoming by looking in a mirror. ("My goodness," said one of my clients after seeing herself on videotape, "I look like a librarian, not a public relations director.") Ben Franklin half-glasses announce "reading," slide down your nose, and make you look old. You're better off wearing bifocals, the top part of which are nonprescription glass. Dark glasses worn indoors can say that you're not comfortable with people, that you're not open, that you're hiding.

Anachronistic or out-of-date clothing—a too-short or too-long skirt when hem lengths are an inch or two inches below the knee—signals, as does out-of-vogue hair length or hair style, that you're not contemporary. When New York's Lieutenant Governor Malcolm Wilson appeared on television in his quest for the governorship, an anachronistically narrow tie and a crew cut announced to prospective voters that he hadn't caught up with today. How could he take care of the state tomorrow?

Polyester double-knit suits, loud ties, light-colored shoes, white socks, socks of any color not high enough to cover the entire shin when you cross your legs equal no authority—or worse. So will succumbing to what Eugenia Sheppard has called the "case of galloping vanity" that's hit men in this country—excessive perfume, hair coloring and permanents, gold chains displayed on hairy chests. At a seminar I gave in Toronto, one man stood out in what he later confessed to me was his effort to be different among conservatively dressed businessmen. He wore running shoes, jogging pants, and a short-sleeved shirt unbuttoned to reveal his furry chest. No one could concentrate on his speech. The inappropriateness of his appearance was distracting. Men should wear only functional jewelry and keep even that simple—avoid flashy cuff links and belt buckles. Collar pins are out-of-date and look bad with wide ties; tie clips, lapel pins, and stickpins do not add to your authority.

Give some thought when you buy a suit to the messages color sends. The darker the color—dark blue and dark gray are best—the greater the authority look.

When you shop for a new suit, take along the items you normally carry in your suit pockets. You'll need that paraphernalia to get your new suit fitted well.

If the trousers of your suit are uncuffed, they should break over the tops of your shoes and be one half to three quarters of an inch longer in back. If you wear cuffs, your trouser hems should be an equal length all around. In either case, the crease should be an unbroken line from belt to toe.

Pay attention to the cut of your shirt collar. If you have a prominent Adam's apple, wear as round and as high a collar as you can find—avoid the V-throated kind. You want attention to be focused on your eyes and face when you speak, not on your bobbing Adam's apple. If your neck is long, look for a collar that's high in back; if your neck is short, you want the opposite. Make sure the collar measurement is your neck measurement. A loose collar makes you look gaunt; a tight collar makes your neck bulge. Avoid button-down collars that have a roll; they tend to look sloppy.

Men who dress impeccably—Sol Linowitz, Dan Rather, Vernon Jordan, and Anwar el-Sadat—wear their shirt cuffs perfectly. Cuffs should end a fraction below the wrist bone and should extend one to two inches beyond your jacket sleeve when you "shoot your cuffs." It's easier to get that right by having your jacket sleeve adjusted to your shirts. If you wear button cuffs, two buttons make for a smoother look than one. Short-sleeved shirts may be more comfortable in summer, but a bare wrist is unflattering and never says "executive" or "professional."

With men's styles changing almost as often as women's, you sometimes may wonder what width tie looks best. The president of a tie company gives this advice: the width of the bottom of the tie, the widest part of the jacket lapel, and the length of the shirt collar from neck to point should all measure the same. The knot of the tie never should be wider than your chin. Because they're bulkier, knitted and woven wool ties generally are not flattering to heavy men or those with large necks. When tied properly, the tip of a tie should come just to your belt buckle. What length you need depends on how tall you are and how you knot your tie. Take a tie that fits you, measure it, and when you buy a new one, make sure it's the same length. But remember, keep more or less in step with the current style.

For a pulled-together look, you can't go wrong with solid colors in your suit and shirt and a small print or striped tie. Rarely can you go wrong with a solid-colored suit and tie and a subtly patterned shirt; that combination is always in good, conservative taste. Play it safe and don't put two patterns together. A quietly patterned shirt and a quietly patterned tie, e.g., a pinstripe shirt and a club tie, might be a place to start experimenting, if you feel your normal look is too drab.

Moustaches are an intriguing subject. I once asked Salvador Dali if he sported his corkscrew moustache to attract attention. "Oh, no," he replied charmingly. "I don't want attention. I really am quite shy. I wear this moustache to distract, not attract. People look at it instead of me." In surveys I've conducted in my seminars, men who wear moustaches say they do so for one of three reasons: to look older, to hide unattractive teeth, to please a wife or girlfriend.

Don't let your moustache upstage you. The droopy Fu Manchu moustache makes its wearer look menacing. The tiny Charlie Chaplin or Hitler variety can give a look of the ridiculous. A moustache usually looks best if it does not come below the corners of the mouth.

One sentence takes care of men's hair: it should be well-groomed and never too far from the prevailing length.

Advice from the Experts on Women's Clothing

A great deal has been written lately about how business and professional women should dress. Some experts recommend a uniform look—gray or navy-blue skirt suit, white blouse, simple pumps, good leather briefcase. I asked Emily Cho, author of *Looking Terrific*, and *Vogue* editor June Weir to give their best advice for the woman who wants to project authority. Miss Cho came up with ten rules:

1. It's important to keep a certain standard of dress, a consistency of style. Don't come to the office one day in a drop-dead suit and show up the next in a cotton-knit T-shirt dress. It's better to buy a few good-quality outfits and change them in small ways (adding a flower at the collar or a scarf, for example) than to have a wardrobe of sleazy clothes.

2. Tie your "professional" outfits together by wearing separate jackets (they don't always have to match your skirt) or vest and weskit layers. Only when your blouse has an important look of its own should you wear it alone with a skirt.

3. Get the core of your wardrobe, i.e., jackets and skirts, in basic colors. That can mean camel, cream, black, but it also could be burgundy, moss green, or mushroom taupe.

4. Your blouse wardrobe is like a man's tie selection. That's where you should have a variety of colors, prints, textures, and collars for visual interest.

5. I'm for slits in skirts even in the office—just sew them down to a decent length so that when you sit you're not overexposed. There's no reason not to use your femininity so long as it's always done in good taste. Soft textures tend to invite human contact and closeness; crisp textures show that a person wants to be regarded as efficient. The lines of clothing, strict or flowing, also convey the same characteristics. If you want to vary your authority image, you can do that with line and texture as well as by type of clothing.

6. The shortest hem length that's appropriate for the office is one inch below your kneecap. On fuller skirt shapes, or if you have wide hips, your skirts should be worn a little longer for grace and balance. The shorter your skirt, the more your legs show, but the bigger your hips will look. Color and fabric weight affect hem length, too. The darker the color or the heavier the fabric, the shorter, by a fraction of an inch or so, you should wear your skirt. With a lightweight fabric like silk or cotton gauze, hems can be worn a bit longer; the fabric gives the skirt a floaty look. If you wear pants, the front hem should touch the top of your shoe, covering the entire instep. The back pants hem should be about a quarter of an inch longer. If your pants are just a shade too short, it will help to match your stocking and shoe color to the color of your pants.

7. Your shoes, handbag, and briefcase also should be in basic colors—tan, brown, black, taupe, or burgundy. A match between shoes and bag needn't be a perfect one, but the color family should be the same. The eye will tend to complete the optical illusion of the nearly matching colors because it wants the two items to go together. You can wear unusual colors—a mauve pump with, say, your black suit, but always balance that with a belt or a small shoulder bag or clutch, or even a hankie, in the same mauve color, or the new color will stick out like a sore thumb.

8. Your hose should be sheer, a neutral skin color, one shade darker than your own skin, and of course seamless and undecorated. It's chic to wear a subtle shade that's a continuation of your skirt color, e.g., sheer pale-gray stockings if you're wearing a gray-flannel skirt.

9. Strict closed pumps may be necessary if you work in a law firm, but an open-toe slingback can add a tremendous amount of femininity without looking unprofessional. Avoid shoes that are very bare or that have stiletto heels.

10. Round gold earrings, two gold chains or a choker, one or two gold bangles make up a good basic jewelry wardrobe for work. Pearls are also professional, if they suit you. Nothing too large or too noisy is the rule.

June Weir takes a somewhat different approach:

"Versatility, comfort, and style are the three key words that make a working woman's wardrobe work.

"Yet it does not mean that a career woman must go out each season and spend lots of money on clothes. Rather, it's important to find a designer or manufacturer who is right for your figure and your way of life. Then, add a couple of looks to your wardrobe or a few replacements each season. Remember, it's better to buy quality than quantity.

"Think about color. Most women make the mistake of buying too many colors for their wardrobe. Think in terms of two or three. Black, navy, gray, and beige are excellent basics for building a working wardrobe. You can adapt an idea that Halston believes in: five easy pieces in one color, a coat, a skirt, a pair of pants, a jacket, a blouse or a sweater. You'll be amazed at the way you can move these pieces around and come up with a look that is polished and professional each time.

"Accessories play an important part in this clean, contemporary look. Start to collect the best basic accessories for business. A variety of small earrings—nothing big or flashy; neat patterns or small round pearls give a dash to solids and neutrals. Your most useful accessory is your watch. Best everyday shapes are square, oval, or round, with a tailored leather band. Collect scarves and mufflers in different lengths, sizes, and fabrics; they're a great addition to your wardrobe.

"The right shoes with the right stockings can make or break your appearance. Generally, closed pumps or slingbacks are best for most offices. Textured and colored pantyhose look great if they work perfectly with your shoes and your clothes. Otherwise, you're better off sticking to a flattering neutral beige.

"Overall it's best to stay away from the obvious: see-through or very tight clothes, a too casual or too dressy look. In a recent survey, personnel directors representing all types of firms, from advertising agencies to insurance companies, agreed that the surest choice for success dressing is a skirt and jacket with a blouse or a dress with a jacket. Not always gray. Not always with a strict white blouse."

If you're a woman working in law or finance or in a very conservative company, you may want to know the "uniform" look that's dictated by John T. Molloy and some other wardrobe experts. The rationale for the look is that a woman who's working in a man's field should take on male protective coloring if she wants to convey authority and professionalism.

The look is simple: a suit (skirt suit, definitely not pant suit) in gray or navy blue, a white blouse for authority (yellow for days when you want to be liked rather than respected), and no vest or weskit (too sexy, because they show bust contours). The collar of the blouse (a standard wing collar, with a maximum of one button open) never should be outside the jacket. Boots and open-toed or open-heeled shoes are out; footwear should be medium-heeled good leather closed pumps and hose skin-colored only. A handbag, if necessary, should be small and of good leather, but it's not so desirable as carrying only a briefcase, in good brown leather. If it's raining, carry a well-made umbrella (at least ten spokes), and never wear a poncho, rain shawl, or plastic rain hat.

Clairol once ran an experiment. They put a group of men in a room behind a one-way mirror and paraded in front of them a bevy of sexy-looking, generously endowed females. Despite the opulence of the young ladies' bosoms, the men's eyes went first to the women's hair. Above all, hair should look neat and well-groomed. Bouncing bangs or hair falling into the eyes is distracting. You want people to look at your eyes and your face when you're with them, not at your hair, not at your hat, not at your dangling earrings.

And not at your neck, either. If you're a woman over twenty-one, or if your neck is long, your eyes and face may be upstaged by the tendons of your neck. A high or a mandarin collar is helpful, as are scarves. Swan-necked Joan Mondale consulted me about speechmaking techniques. She left with a piece of advice that helped her keep audience attention, to switch from V-necked to mandarin-collared dresses or to wear scarves. Turtleneck sweaters, ruffles and bows at the neck, beads that fill in the neckline also are useful camouflage. Avoid chokers, which emphasize.

If you have a short neck, which usually goes with a round face, avoid jewel-necked Peter Pan collars and high choker necklaces. Hanging necklaces will lengthen the dimension of your face and neck. V-necks are good on you, as are wide U-necks; avoid high ruffles. If your jacket collar sits slightly away from the back of your neck, your neck will look longer.

If you're tall and thin, avoid the bare or clinging. Look for fullness and softness in cut and in material. Vertically striped patterns are not for you. Layering adds interest and disguises over-thinness.

If you're short, a single color and simple lines are best; avoid horizontal stripes or patterns. Never clutter your neck; that makes you look dumpy. Avoid ankle straps or heavy shoes because they will call attention downward and make your legs look shorter; avoid anything but plain hose for the same reason.

If you ought to lose a few pounds but haven't got around to it yet, some tricks of dressing can make you look thinner. Wear a single color or tones of a single-color family. Your skirt should be slim rather than full, or with soft gathering at the center front and back. Stay away from oversized anything—collars, shoulders, bulky layers, or pants cuffs—that detract from a vertical line. A shorter jacket gives a leggier appearance. Buy clothes that are a little loose rather than a little tight. Too tight makes you look uncomfortable and heavier than you are. An exception is the jacket that you never intend to wear closed; that can fit more snugly and help make you look trimmer.

Whatever your body shape, your clothes should fit properly and neatly. A jacket that's perfectly tailored will look too big for you if the sleeves are even a half inch too long; the sleeve should be just long enough to cover the top of the wristbone, letting your blouse cuff peek out about an inch.

Makeup

Cosmetics can enhance or detract; they should be used judiciously. Janet was a well-groomed, perfectly dressed executive, except for the glistening green eye shadow she wore as thick as toothpaste. Every morning, she said, she tried to use less, but she was hooked: the eye shadow, she believed, drew attention away from her large nose. In fact, the eye shadow was not doing all that well at distracting attention from her nose, but it was a huge success at detracting from Janet's brains and charm. If she could let those qualities come through, people would be far less likely to notice her nose.

Speaking of noses, Anne Morrow Lindbergh tells this story about her mother. When her daughters were very little, Mrs. Morrow gave a high tea at which the senior J. P. Morgan was to be one of the guests. The children were to be brought in, introduced, and ushered out. Mrs. Morrow's great fear was that Anne, the most outspoken of her daughters, might comment audibly on Mr. Morgan's celebrated and conspicuous nose. She therefore took pains to explain to Anne that personal observations were impolite and to caution her especially against commenting on Mr. Morgan's nose, no matter what. When the moment came and the girls were brought in, Mrs. Morrow held her breath as she saw Anne fix her gaze unfalteringly on the objective and remain there. Nevertheless, the introductions were made, the little girls curtsied and were sent on their way. With a sigh of relief, Mrs. Morrow turned back to her duties as hostess and asked her chief guest, "And now, Mr. Morgan, will you have cream or lemon in your nose?"

People often trade one distractor for another. A celebrated statesman had a very crooked front tooth, and because of it he hardly ever smiled in public. On those rare occasions when he did, he covered his upper teeth with his lip. I suggested to him that he evaluate the cost of hiding that tooth—that grim smile was giving him a reputation as a cold and haughty man. When he opened his lips and loosened up into a grin, his charm was so dazzling, no one noticed his tooth (which was not, of course, all that terrible).

3

Getting Your Speaking Act Together

The Most Unforgettable Client I Ever Met was a short, chunky man who arrived unheralded at my office door wearing a bright plaid suit and a gaudy tie with a diamond stickpin. His brow was beaded with perspiration.

"Ya gotta help me, ya gotta help me," he gasped. "I gotta give a fi' minute talk acceptin' an award on Sadday night at a dinna. I'm a bail bondsman and none of dem criminals make me noivous, but that audience—I'm scared to death."

Some of the most sophisticated people in the world also quake at the idea of facing an audience. Captains of industry who are giants at their desks become pygmies on a podium; chairmen of the board self-destruct at stockholders' meetings. And today, more than ever, the ability to speak well in public is a critical one for those in business. "On the list of executive skills," reports the New York *Times*, "public speaking has become virtually a must. With the visibility of business leadership in the media increasing, executives often have to appear at public forums, before Congressional hearings, and at conventions."

According to *The Book of Lists*, speaking before a group heads the list of the fourteen worst human fears (beating out heights, financial problems, insects, deep water, sickness, death, and flying, in that order). But happily, that fear can be conquered, and with considerably more ease than one client of mine experienced. Before he came to me, he had spent nine years in analysis trying to overcome his fear of public speaking. Our program did for him in four hours what nine years on the couch could not.

Delivering a good talk well—and doing that without the nervousness that can ruin it—requires two separate operations: preparing your material—thoroughly; and preparing yourself—thoroughly. Speechmaking confidence comes from knowing that you have something worth saying, and that you can say it in a way that's worth listening to.

Controlling nervousness begins with anticipation—one of the most valuable processes of our daily lives, and one of the least often used consciously. You anticipate every time you cross a street: What if that car turns sharply? Can I make it across before the light changes? Anticipation also can make the difference between success and disaster in less mundane matters. When a professional golfer tees off at a tournament, he has already considered all his alternatives. What's the best way out of the sand trap on the fifth hole? What if the wind shifts? Like him, you can avoid unpleasant consequences by intelligent appraisal.

KNOWING YOUR AUDIENCE

The night I opened in a play in Philadelphia, Noel Coward came backstage to my dressing room to wish me well. "Noel," I asked, "what are these Philadelphia audiences like?" "Well," he said, "we did a preview for the Veterans Hospital. That night we played for the wounded. The next night we opened and played for the dead."

When you've agreed to give a talk, whether to a boardroom full of colleagues or to thousands of people at an annual stockholders' meeting, your first task is intelligent anticipation. Size up the situation.

First, learn all you can about the audience. A group of business executives and a group of high school students require entirely different approaches even if the subject of the speech is the same. Know your audience's frame of reference. When, in 1978, I was consulted by Prime Minister Begin's staff, I discussed our two cultures' different interpretations of the same phrase. "When he answers a question by saying, 'It's for our survival,' " I said, "that phrase to an American means food and shelter; it doesn't mean what it means to an Israeli—non-annihilation."

"We never thought of it that way," they said.

President Reagan demonstrated how well he knew his audience in the summation of his debate with President Carter. Most people agreed that up to that point the candidates were neck and neck. But it was the brilliant perception of the personal concerns of the American people, as well as the powerful writing and the cadence and rhythm of those four straight-to-the-heart-and-soul questions, that made Ronald Reagan the winner in that contest:

Are you better off than you were four years ago?
Is it easier for you to go and buy things in the store than it was four years ago?
Is America as respected throughout the world as we were four years ago?
Do you feel that our security is as safe? That we are as strong as we were four years ago?

Find out from the person who booked you the average age and socioeconomic level of your audience, as well as their interests, prejudices, and political inclinations. Are there topics you should avoid? One speaker opened with a joke about plane crashes, not knowing that the wife of the meeting's chairman recently had been killed in one. He had not researched his audience. A famous hairdresser emptied an auditorium full of executive wives in twenty minutes. He laced his speech too liberally with obscenities. "If we do our best for the audience," said Alan Alda, explaining the success of "M*A*S*H" despite its controversial subjects and high standards, "they'll let us do it any way we can."

How many people will be there? You can take a more casual approach with a small audience. The larger the group, the more energy and enthusiasm you need to generate.

How large is the room in which you'll be speaking? Will there be a standing lectern (my preference)? If you'll be using visual aids, describe to your contact what you'll need—an easel, projector, operator.

Find out which past speakers and what prior topics have succeeded in front of the same audience, and why. If other speakers are appearing with you, and if you have a choice of the order in which you'll speak, be first. That way you eliminate the chance that your material will be covered before you can deliver it.

Find out how long your talk should be, and honor your time limit. (One of those key-chain timers that reminds you when your parking meter is about to expire can be useful. Set the timer to go off two minutes before the scheduled end of your speech, and it will buzz to tell you it's time to move into your conclusion.) If the length of time is left up to you, fifteen or twenty minutes is long enough for a talk that's the main event at a luncheon or dinner; forty minutes or so is right at a mealless meeting.

Remember, half as long may be twice as good. President William Henry Harrison not only bored his listeners to death at his inaugural in 1841 with his hour-and-a-half-long address, he literally talked himself to death too. It was a freezing, rainy day, he caught a bad cold and a month later died of pneumonia.

Two more reminders: Find out whether there will be a question and answer period. Aim to have one. I'd rather do without my makeup than without a Q & A. What day of the week and what time of the day do you speak? Speeches made in the morning and at the beginning of the week require more energy and momentum than those made later in the day and week.

INTRODUCTION INSURANCE

When Northwestern University's dean escorted Patricia Neal on stage and attempted to introduce her, the graduating seniors of the school of speech went wild. They welcomed their chosen convocation speaker with such a roar of applause and cheers that the dean had no chance of being heard.

Pat Neal, as an alumna of the school, represented this group as no one else could have. The drama students cheered her accomplishments in their chosen field. The speech therapists understood her victory over a dreadful stroke and loved her for it.

The dean stood at the microphone and waited. Finally the welcome subsided to a milder din, and the dean was able to make himself heard. He looked at Pat and then back at the students. "I'm supposed to make an introduction," he said, "but I see that you have met."

That is about the only circumstance in which you need not bother to send the chairperson a brief (about 150 words) suggested introduction. Don't be modest. Introducers are usually grateful not to have to take the time to write one. And you'll avoid having your credentials confused or omitted. Or worse: "Richard Swann is giving his delightful talk for us this evening on behalf of the International Relief Fund. His services are free. I am sure that, knowing this, we will all feel that coming to hear him has been worth it."

An introduction should heighten audience interest in both speaker and topic. Humor, human interest, and warmth all can be used, with restraint. You might send an introduction like this one:

> Our speaker today has seen action on both sides of the lines. For eight years he has served with distinction as a member of the greatest auditing firm in the world, the United States Internal Revenue Service. For eighteen years, he's worked as a key member of the internal audit staff of Olsen Brothers. Prior to his IRS postgraduate work in duplicity avoidance, evasion, and chicanery, he attended Saint Joseph's University, where he earned high honors in both the financial and football fields. Despite his constant exposure to human weakness, our guest maintains a personal life that has survived twenty-seven years of audits. We are happy to welcome Russ Canfield.

A SPEECH WITH COLOR

A good speech is almost as rare as a good speaker. When President Carter and I were about to work on his Cuba speech at Camp David, Mrs. Carter walked in. "What do you think about the speech, Rosalynn?" the President asked her.

"Most of it's pretty strong," she said, "but an awful lot of it's very weak."

After the President and I had finished working, Susan Clough asked if I had time to meet with Mrs. Carter. I said I would be delighted.

"Hello, First Lady?" Mrs. Clough trilled over the phone. "Miss First Lady? Why don't you and Dorothy have a cup of coffee for a few minutes? You two can talk over some things about the President's speeches."

"What do we need?" Mrs. Carter asked when we met in the lounge. She was warm and friendly and concerned.

"The most important thing a speech needs is good speechwriting," I said.

A President's statements are always subject to excruciating analysis and interpretation by Congress, the media, the citizens, nations friendly and unfriendly. If it's a choice between clarity in unimaginative wording and possible ambiguity in well-turned phrases, the former always wins. Perhaps a President's speeches have to be colorless, but since it's unlikely your words are in danger of being misinterpreted by the whole world, your talks don't have to be dull. They won't be if you follow some simple guidelines.

Preparation is the step that follows anticipation. When you've learned all you can about the setting of your talk and about your audience, lay the groundwork for your talk. First, define your objective. What information or message do you want to leave with the audience? What action do you want them to take after you've finished speaking, besides applaud you? Do you want to inform, persuade, or entertain—or all three?

An informative talk adds to its listeners' knowledge but isn't intended to change or strengthen opinions. It simply may be the extended and orderly answer to some factual question: "How does a fluctuating prime rate affect our business?" "Why have college board scores been dropping?" "What should you pack for a trip to Europe?" A persuasive talk, by contrast, presents a problem, proposes solutions and, through a progression of carefully reasoned steps, rouses its listeners to action.

A former First Lady's secretary was invited by a top lecture bureau to join its lucrative circuit. She hesitated, not wanting to reveal state secrets. We defined her objective—to inform and entertain without violating confidences or being a gossip. And then we were able to structure her talk—around the differences between the public's glamour image of a press secretary's job and the reality. We could weave in a judiciously chosen group of anecdotes but keep the talk from becoming a series of unrelated and pointless stories.

The focus of your talk is critical. Write it down in a phrase or sentence. "Save energy." "Contribute to your community fund." "How to cut operating costs." Print those few words on an index card and keep that card in sight as you write your speech. Think of the phrase as a goalpost on a football field. Each idea and sentence should advance your speech toward the goal line. If it doesn't, toss it out.

Organization Is the Key

Next, begin to collect your material—background, anecdotes, studies, statistical data. If your topic concerns your company or organization, you have ready sources of information. But what if your subject is further from home? Reference librarians are almost uniformly helpful, and a little thought should suggest other resources. If your talk is about travel, for instance, the American Society of Travel Agents might have useful studies from which you could quote. National consumer groups make it their business to have up-to-date statistics about consumerism. Alert your family and friends to keep their eyes open for relevant items in newspapers, magazines, and books.

Keep your material organized from the start. If you just toss things into a folder and hope to create order later, you'll be faced with a discouraging mess when you start to prepare your talk. Label and use separate folders: Introduction; Body of talk; Conclusion. Or even finer distinctions: History; Current practices; What others think; Trends; Controversy. Keep relevant quotations and anecdotes in a separate folder. And collect them avidly —they're the mustard and relish on the hotdog.

The thinking part of your writing also should begin as soon as you've accepted. Mull over what you want to say as you commute or jog or wait for an elevator. As you know, good ideas can strike anywhere, any time. If you're not already in the habit of keeping a notebook handy, do that now.

Put another next to your bed. My favorite time for speech gestation lies just between sleeping and waking. My mind seems to be most creative in those twilight or dawn moments. Deliberately, before dropping off at night or coming fully awake in the morning, I mull over ideas for a talk. During the day I consider the possibilities at odd moments, avoiding any sense of pressure. Then sud-

denly, often when I least expect it, I feel the little mental kick that
signals an idea about to surface. If the kick comes during the
night, I grope for the pad on my nightstand.

Begin the actual preparation of your talk at least three weeks before its delivery date. Waiting until the last minute is disastrous.
Good, economical writing is an arduous and time-consuming job—
plan on at least a half hour of writing time for every minute of
speaking time. (Mark Twain once apologized to a friend for writing so long a letter; he hadn't had time, he said, to write a shorter
one.)

Your speech is divided into opening remarks, body, and conclusion. Most people prepare, or at least organize, the body of their
speech before deciding how to introduce it, since it's easier to
develop an introduction when you know what idea you're intro-
ducing. Some people prefer to begin at the beginning—or even at
the end. We'll open, for simplicity's sake, with the opening.

Openings for Attention

The varieties of opening remarks are as limitless as your imagination. Begin with something unexpected, or a remark about local
characteristics, problems, or events that gets audience interest.

Begin with a question ("How many of you had cereal for breakfast this morning?"). Make a dramatic statement: cite an incident
from the day's news, from history, from your own life. Use an apt
quotation. These devices create instant interest. (For examples of
excellent openings, see Appendix.)

Avoid those tired old roll calls: "Mister president, ladies and
gentlemen, honored guests, it's a privilege and a pleasure . . ." Everybody knows who's in the room. You want to capture the audience's attention from the start. I once began a talk before an audience of international corporation presidents: "Good morning to all
of you personable, peripatetic, prepossessing, perceptive, persuasive, particular, purposeful, prestigious, persevering, polished,
practical, productive, and powerful presidents." I got that out on
one breath at tongue-twisting speed, and the audience loved it.

No matter how compelling it is, resist the impulse to start with
an apology. (Why do so many people say, "I'm not a speech-
maker," and then insist on proving it?) Doing so only alerts the
audience to look for shortcomings. Misplaced modesty can sabo-

tage your speech. If you begin by saying in effect, "I'm not really good enough to be on this platform," your audience will listen for evidence to back up your self-assessment.

Humor can make a memorable introduction, as in the following examples:

> I recently read that the preamble to the Declaration of Independence contains three hundred words; the Ten Commandments, ninety-seven; the Gettysburg Address, two hundred and sixty-seven, and the Lord's Prayer fewer than a hundred. However, a recent report from the federal government on the pricing of cabbages allegedly contains twenty-six thousand, nine hundred and eleven words. I will confine my remarks to something between the Lord's Prayer and the price of cabbages.

Or:

> Looking around at all of you in this distinguished group, I feel like a mongrel entered in the Westminster Kennel Club Show. He may not win, but he's in damn fine company.

A word of warning about humor. Use it only if it comes easily to you (and also assuming, of course, that humor is suitable for the audience and the occasion). A joke that falls flat is death. Try out any humor on your friends first. If they don't laugh, your jokes won't fare any better when a hundred or a thousand people are listening.

The Heart of the Matter

With your introduction, you make friends with your audience. In your conclusion, you bring down the curtain on your act. But the heart of your talk is where you develop your theme and convince your listeners.

The body of a speech that is designed to inform should be composed of a progression of points in logical sequence, connected by transitions that enable the audience to follow shifts of thought. Every sentence should be germane to the short phrase written on your index card that's the focus of your speech, and every sentence should lead inexorably to your conclusion. If your objective is simply to entertain, you can forget logic, but don't forget organization.

In a persuasive talk, present the problem and line up the proposed solutions. Remember that you're a salesman. Through a series of carefully reasoned steps, move the listeners to action, each step leading logically to the next, linked by a smooth transition.

No matter what kind of talk you're writing, several simple rules apply:

Keep it simple. At a gathering of mathematicians, someone attempted to explain Einstein's theories. After the mathematician had run on for over an hour, a listener interrupted him. "I think," said the fellow, "that you are greater than Einstein himself. Twelve men understand Einstein, but nobody understands you."

Don't clutter your talk. A listener can't pause and reflect over long and complicated sentences the way a reader can. If your audience has to backtrack mentally, you lose their attention. Avoid words and phrases that force a listener to remember what went before, like "it" too far from its antecedent, "formerly," or "the latter." Use numbers (other than statistics—did you hear about the fellow who drowned in a stream that had an average depth of six inches?—and percentages) sparingly. Avoid jargon and technical language unless it's readily understood by your audience. Keep your sentences short for comprehension. Mark Twain once said that a spoken sentence of more than seventeen words usually loses listeners.

Write for the tongue. Spoken language is different from written language. A talk, whether to thirty people or to three thousand, should have the quality of speaking not at or to, but with and for. The best speeches seem like one side of a conversation, enlarged. They sound the way a person sounds when he's discussing the subject heatedly over a dinner table. That means spoken speech, your usual vocabulary, and simple phrases.

Make sure the words and sentences you write are right for your tongue. When, in rehearsal for *The King and I,* I tripped on a line twice, Oscar Hammerstein said, "If your tongue trips the second time you try to speak it, I've written it wrong." Say your sentences aloud from time to time, and rewrite any sentence you've stumbled over more than once.

Use contractions freely—they make your speech less stilted and more effective. Don't be afraid to use a preposition at the end of a sentence, and don't be scared of colloquial English. You use the words "I," "we," and "you," constantly in conversation; use them when you're writing a talk. Try not to slip into the passive voice: "It will be seen . . ." "It is assumed . . ." Using personal pronouns and the active voice makes your speech more forceful and immediate.

Figures of speech, which you doubtless recall from high school English, also can add color to a speech. Alliteration, the repetition of initial sounds in a series of words, captures the attention ("dedicated, devoted directors," "profitable proliferation of potential") and puts music into a sentence. Anaphora, the repetition of the same words at the beginning of consecutive phrases, is a favorite of the most compelling speakers. An example is Winston Churchill's famous exhortation: "We shall fight on the beaches, we shall fight on the landing grounds, we shall fight in the fields and in the streets, we shall fight in the hills; we shall never surrender." Anaphora works as well for ordinary speakers as it does for famous orators.

Color through anecdotes. Personal stories appropriately used hold audience interest as nothing else can. The president of a conglomerate underlined his humanness by referring in a talk to his youth in a run-down neighborhood: "My hero was the kid who could hit a ball three sewers."

Quotations and anecdotes are point-makers that attract and inform. "I quote others only the better to express myself," said Montaigne. Use analogies to bring home your points. Engage your listeners' visual senses whenever possible. Saying, "The work area measures five thousand square feet," is better than saying, "The work area is enormous." But neither is so good as saying, "The work area is the size of our local football field." When I consulted with Prime Minister Begin's staff, I told them it was their job to supply the Prime Minister for his appearances in this country with analogies Americans could understand. "If you describe Israel at its narrowest point by saying, 'Israel is so narrow that we can be attacked,' the Americans won't get it," I said. "Instead say, 'Israel is so narrow that if you were driving on an American highway, it would take you only twenty minutes to get from one end of Israel to the other.'"

If you use a generalization, back it up with a specific the mind's eye can see. So, too, with abstractions. Inflation comes to life for a listener not in terms of billion-dollar items but of the cost of a quart of milk.

Clinching Closers

Like a love affair and a three-act play, a talk is easily begun; ending it requires considerable skill. If you fade out, you dilute the reaction to an otherwise compelling talk. Even an adequate talk is vastly improved by a strong closing flourish.

Quotations often make excellent closings. For a charity appeal, I once used this:

> These were the last lines written by Oscar Hammerstein. He wrote them just before he entered the hospital for the last time:
>
>> A song is no song 'til you sing it
>> A bell is no bell 'til you ring it
>> And love in your heart
>> Wasn't put there to stay
>> Love isn't love
>> 'Til you give it away.

Then I paused and concluded: "I thank you for giving your time and your love to this great cause today."

A stirring speech merits a stirring conclusion, like this one:

> As you enter the arena, ask yourself, "Do I want to settle for the big, soft nothingness of the middle road? Or do I want to try for the top, take risks, and do something important? Do I want my life to be productive, exhilarating, and enriching—an adventure?" If your answer is yes, then you've got to go out there and take risks. For without the element of risk and chance, life is dull. Fulfillment, excitement, and happiness await you if you let every summit be a valley to a peak beyond.

An equally effective climax is the diminuendo, or dissolve ending, "irising-out," so to speak. In staging a song that conveys deep emotion and ends on a low key, a "soul song," the spotlight on the singer gradually diminishes to a pinpoint and disappears with the last note of the song. So, in the intensity of an emotional ending to a speech:

> So far we've done our job exceptionally well. Thousands of uncommon men and women have made our company a success. Ralph Waldo Emerson once said that there were five keys to suc-

cess: To leave the world a bit better by a job well done or a redeemed social condition. To win the respect of intelligent people, to earn the appreciation of critics. To find the best in others. And to know that even one life has breathed easier, because you have lived.

The final words fade like that spotlight, for a moment holding the listeners emotionally suspended. (For additional examples of well-formed finales, see the Appendix.)

One last warning—don't try something too dramatic for you. Franz Liszt is said to have paid women to faint at his concerts. The swoon always was timed to occur just before the climax of his most popular cadenza. Liszt would leap from his piano stool, pick up the swooner, and leave the rest of the audience impressed by his brilliance and dismayed by their own stolidity. Once, however, the hired fainter forgot to faint. As Liszt's fingers flew up the keys, he discovered he could not finish the run. So he fainted himself.

GUIDELINES FROM THE EXPERTS

Although I used this material in my earlier book, there still is no better set of principles for writing a speech than those outlined by Theodore Sorensen, in his description of the working relationship between himself and President John F. Kennedy:

> We were not conscious of following the elaborate techniques later ascribed to these speeches by literary analysts. Neither of us had any special training in composition, linguistics, or semantics. Our chief criterion was always audience comprehension and comfort, and this meant: (1) short speeches, short clauses, and short words, wherever possible; (2) a series of points or propositions in numbered or logical sequence, wherever appropriate; and (3) the construction of sentences, phrases and paragraphs in such a manner as to simplify, clarify, and emphasize.
>
> The test of a text was not how it appeared to the eye but how it sounded to the ear. His best paragraphs, when read aloud, often had a cadence not unlike blank verse—indeed at times key words would rhyme. He was fond of alliterative sentences, not solely for reasons of rhetoric but to reinforce the audience's recollection of his reasoning . . .
>
> Words were regarded as tools of precision, to be chosen and applied with a craftsman's care to whatever the situation re-

quired. He liked to be exact. But if the situation required a certain vagueness, he would deliberately choose a word of varying interpretations rather than bury his imprecision in ponderous prose.

For he disliked verbosity and pomposity in his own remarks as much as he disliked them in others. He wanted both his message and his language to be plain and unpretentious, but never patronizing. He wanted his major policy statements to be positive, specific and definite, avoiding the use of "suggest," "perhaps" and "possible alternatives for consideration" . . .

He used little or no slang, dialect, legalistic terms, contractions, clichés, elaborate metaphors, or ornate figures of speech. He refused to be folksy or to include any phrase or image he considered corny, tasteless or trite. He rarely used words he considered hackneyed: "humble," "dynamic," "glorious." He used none of the customary word fillers (e.g., "And I say to you that is a legitimate question and here is my answer"). And he did not hesitate to depart from strict rules of English usage when he thought adherence to them (e.g., "Our agenda *are* long") would grate on the listener's ear . . .

He believed topical, tasteful, pertinent, pointed humor at the beginning of his remarks to be a major means of establishing audience rapport; and he would work with me as diligently for the right opening witticism, or take as much pride the next day in some spontaneous barb he had flung, as he would on the more substantive paragraphs in his text.

Combine that advice with the suggestions made by Jock Elliott, chairman of Ogilvy & Mather, and one of the most superb speakers I've ever heard, and you will have a complete manual of speechwriting:

Last month I got a letter from a vice-president of a major management consultant firm. Let me read you two paragraphs. The first:

"Recently, the companies of our Marketing Services Group were purchased by one of the largest consumer research firms in the United States. While this move well fits the business purpose and focus of the acquired MSG units, it is personally restrictive. I will rather choose to expand my management opportunities with a career move into industry."

What he meant was: "The deal works fine for my company,

but not so fine for me. I'm looking for another job." Second paragraph:

"The base of managerial and technical accomplishment reflected in my enclosed résumé may suggest an opportunity to meet a management need for one of your clients. Certainly my experience promises a most productive pace to understand the demands and details of any new situation I would choose."

What he meant was: "As you can see in my résumé, I've had a lot of good experience. I am a quick study. Do you think any of your clients might be interested in me?"

At least that's what I think he meant. This fellow's letter reveals him as a pompous ass. He may not *be* a pompous ass. He may be only a terrible writer. But I haven't the interest or time to find out which. There are so many people looking for jobs who *don't* sound like pompous asses. Bad writing did him in—with me, at any rate.

Our written and spoken words reflect what we are. If our words are brilliant, precise, well-ordered, and human, then that is how we are seen. If our words are dull, murky, disordered, and pompous, that is how we are seen.

When you write, you must constantly ask yourself: What am I trying to say? If you do this religiously, you will be surprised at how often you don't know what you are trying to say.

You have to *think* before you start every sentence, and you have to *think* about every word. Then you must look at what you have written and ask: Have I said it? Is it clear to someone encountering the subject for the first time? If it's not, that is because some fuzz has worked its way into the machinery. The clear writer is a person clearheaded enough to see this stuff for what it is: fuzz. You cannot write clearly unless you think clearly first.

It is not easy to write a simple declarative sentence. Here is one way to do it. Think what you want to say. Write your sentence. Then strip it of all adverbs and adjectives. Reduce the sentence to its skeleton. Let the verbs and nouns do the work.

If your skeleton sentence does not express your thought precisely, you've got the wrong verb or noun. Dig for the right one. Nouns and verbs carry the guns in good writing; adjectives and adverbs are decorative camp followers.

If you have written something that takes eight pages, try rewriting it in four. This will force you to think, force you to remove repetitive clutter, force you to simplify. I'll guarantee it will be better in four pages.

Then comes the hard part. Rewrite it in three. Simplify. Simplify.

When you rewrite—and rewrite you must—remember how the words you are stringing together *sound*. They should sound good, have a rhythm to them. Even more important, they should sound like *you*. You must use words and expressions that are natural to you. The listener must say to himself, "Yes, that's Charlie, all right."

The greatest writers have always slaved over their work. Charles Dickens was one of the most sublime, prolific story-tellers of all time. How effortlessly the tales seemed to flow from his pen. But how effortless was it? If you were to look at the first manuscript page of the masterpiece *A Christmas Carol,* the first two sentences are clean. From there on, almost every sentence was improved by Dickens' second thoughts, his editing.

Earlier I suggested that what you write in eight pages you should cut to four. And then to three. Perhaps you think that is impossible, that I was exaggerating to make a point. I turn to Dickens again.

His annual tour of the United States was a theatrical highlight each year. One of his most popular readings was of *A Christmas Carol.* In the interest of time, he had to *cut it in less than half.*

Yes, it is possible to cut *your* immortal words—and mine—in half, and then some.

I can only say Hallelujah and Amen to Mr. Elliott and add a few small points about editing a talk.

YOUR BEST EDITOR, THE TAPE RECORDER

If a written communication is best polished on paper, a speech is best edited by the ear. Read the first draft of your speech into a tape recorder. Don't bother with your delivery now; this reading is for the purpose of evaluating and improving content, not style. Imagine that you're listening to a stranger's speech on the radio. (Turn your back to the tape recorder. It will help you be objective.) As you listen, you may find yourself saying, "I wish he'd get to the point," or, "That's irrelevant." Ask yourself whether his speech makes sense, whether the transitions are smooth. Do the words sound like spoken speech? Is there anything missing, any redundancy?

Edit and tighten your speech at least four times. Space the sessions a day or two apart to refresh your objectivity. Try constantly to pare out unneeded words. I am thoroughly opposed to the "Tell them what you're going to tell them; tell them what you want to tell them; tell them what you told them" school of speechwriting.

Edit for length as well as for strength—otherwise you may find yourself in the position of one speaker who wandered on endlessly as listeners slipped away. Outside in the lobby, one of the last fugitives met an earlier escapee who asked, "Has he finished yet?" "Yes," said the man who had just left, "long ago. But he doesn't know it."

Check your final draft against this editing checklist:

1. Have I honored all requirements of the talk?

2. Have I researched the topic enough? Investigated all sources?

3. Have I taken into account the nature of the audience—its socioeconomic level, degree of sophistication and culture, age, sex, experience?

4. Have I familiarized myself with the locale, its idioms, and news?

5. Have I rechecked to make sure the talk fits the allotted time?

6. Have I tailored the scope of the topic for the time allotted?

7. Have I constructed the talk so that it has a clear purpose, makes a point, and comes to a conclusion?

8. Have I enough strong ideas in the talk, and have I developed them sufficiently?

9. Have I arranged the points in a good order?

10. Have I asked questions, used "you" enough?

11. Have I an appropriate introduction?

12. Have I a strong conclusion?

13. Have I enough variety, specifics, and continuity?

14. Does my language appeal to sight, sound, smell, taste, and touch?

15. Have I used too many numbers or statistics?

16. Have I prepared the speech in spoken, not written, language?

4

Practice Like a Pro

The unspoken prayer of almost everyone who gets up on his feet to speak in public echoes these lines from Isaiah 55:11:

> So shall my word be that goeth forth out of my mouth: it shall not return unto me void, but it shall accomplish that which I please, and it shall prosper in the thing whereto I sent it.

Prayers may help, but you're giving the responsibility to God. Security comes from knowing you can do it yourself. The reason there are so few good speakers in public is that there are so few good rehearsers in private.

Think of the speakers you've heard who were so magnetic your attention never wandered, and of the speakers (inevitably a much longer list) who bored or disappointed you. Compelling speakers have warmth, enthusiasm, animation, intensity—energy. They keep eye contact with their audience and inspire trust; you believe what they're saying. Bad speakers, by contrast, seem cold, insincere, wooden. Engaging speakers seem at ease with themselves; an air of confidence, authority, and conviction makes an audience relax and feel receptive. Poor speakers, on the other hand, appear wretchedly nervous; listening to them is an ordeal.

One of the most important steps in taking yourself out of the second category of speakers and into the first is what I call Familiarization. That's the process of getting your talk off the paper and into yourself, and then out of yourself and into your audience.

There are three reasons why President Reagan delivers speeches effectively: his speeches are well written; as a former actor he knows how to phrase; and, most important, he knows the value of rehearsal. Before his nomination acceptance and inaugural speeches he holed up in his Virginia garage with cameras and Teleprompters and rehearsed and rehearsed and rehearsed. Before the big debate, he did the same.

Look at the word "rehearse." Cross out the last two letters and you're left with the word REHEAR. Rehearing is what rehearsing is all about. You should not hear your talk for the first time in front of an audience. Simply looking over what you plan to say doesn't substitute for saying it, any more than reading about faraway places substitutes for a visit. I can't say it too often: Rehearse as if you were in the real-life situation. On your feet. Aloud. Seeing the most skeptical of faces in front of you.

Should you read your talk? Memorize it? Speak from an outline, notes, or cue cards? Each method has its advantages and drawbacks. A few spellbinders can speak without referring to a text of any kind. President Kennedy was one of them; Reginald Jones, former chief executive of General Electric, and John Connolly are two others. But those men had or have the gift of a photographic memory.

If you memorize, your eyes look glazed. It robs you of valuable eye contact with the audience. If you read from a prepared text and deliver your speech to the lectern, you may as well stay home and send a cassette.

Cue words or phrases can make you grope and ramble. You have to search for words and write your sentences at the lectern, instead of concentrating solely on your delivery and playing to your audience. Cue users lose urgency, intensity, and momentum; they tend to wander from the subject. Your job on the podium is to *deliver* the talk, not to create it. You can be sure that "I have nothing to offer but blood, toil, tears and sweat" was not coined by Churchill at the lectern.

The best way to deliver a speech is to have your full text in front of you, but in such a form that you can talk it, not read it, permitting you to be eye-to-eye with your listeners 80 percent of the time.

CREATING A LECTERN SCRIPT

Start with a complete word-for-word text of your talk. While reading the words aloud, make a slash mark with a red pen or pencil wherever you naturally take a breath. Generally, that will be at the ends of phrases and sentences. You should have something like this:

> Let's start with the premise/that a private company is in business to make money./It doesn't always work out that way,/but that's the object of the game./Now, it's certainly possible to lose money/even with plenty of customers./But it's flatly impossible to make money/with no customers at all./
> So our business needs customers./And if we plan to stay in business very long,/we need more than just "customers,"/we need satisfied customers.

Now retype the final speech in capital letters for easy visibility. (If you're hand-printing, do it on lined paper, using a black felt-tip pen. Make the letters one line high.) Write only one phrase to a line, and skip a line between. Use abbreviations, but never past instant comprehension. Your script should look something like this:

LET'S START WITH THE PREMISE
THAT A PRIVATE CO. IS IN BIZ TO MAKE MONEY.
IT DOESN'T ALWAYS WORK OUT THAT WAY,
BUT THAT'S THE OBJECT OF THE GAME.
NOW IT'S CERTAINLY POSSIBLE TO LOSE MONEY
EVEN WITH PLENTY OF CUSTOMERS.
BUT IT'S FLATLY IMPOSSIBLE TO MAKE MONEY
WITH NO CUSTOMERS AT ALL.
SO OUR BIZ NEEDS CUSTOMERS.
& IF WE PLAN TO STAY IN BIZ VERY LONG,
WE NEED MORE THAN JUST "CUSTOMERS,"
WE NEED SATISFIED CUSTOMERS.

To see how this interim script works, you'll have to get up on your feet and pretend you're at a lectern. (Using a lectern will not make you come across pompous or remote. A lectern can be to a speaker what a pedestal is to sculpture. It enhances you and gives importance to what you're saying. A lectern also anchors you and keeps you from pacing.) Make a practice lectern by piling up phone books and dictionaries on a table in front of a mirror. The mirror will help you check your platform demeanor as you speak. Pile the books high enough so that when you look into a mirror over the books, you see yourself from the bottom of your ribcage up.

Standing at the lectern, read the opening two phrases of your interim script over and over to yourself, visually soaking them up. Stamp those phrases on your mind. Now, speak the lines aloud, so that you hear the cadence of the phrases. That gives you aural as well as visual recall.

Look into your own eyes in the mirror as you talk. Keep the index finger of your left hand moving down the lefthand margin of the page as you speak. Your finger will guide your eyes to where they will pick up your next phrase.

Here's the rhythm of what you're doing (try to keep it flowing): Finger points to the place where your eyes go. Scoop up the phrase. Eyes go to mirror. Deliver. Finger moves to the next line. Scoop up the phrase. Eyes go to mirror. Deliver.

Practice with your interim lectern script until you've developed the smooth-flowing rhythm of a swimmer doing the Australian crawl.

Now take it one step further. Imagine the audience in the mirror is three people—yourself and one person on either side of you. Read the script again, eye-sweeping from person to person to person, scooping a phrase and delivering it to the eyes of the person to your left, your own eyes, the eyes of the person on your right. The action of your eyes should be one smooth, gentle motion, like the action of a horizontal windshield wiper, sweeping across and then sweeping back.

ANNOTATING YOUR LECTERN SCRIPT

Now mark up the interim script to make it your lectern script. This will help give more color, momentum, and emphasis to your delivery. For moderate emphasis, use hyphens between words:

THERE IS NOTHING-WE-CANNOT-ACHIEVE!

For stronger emphasis, use hypens between words and a wavy line under the phrase:

THERE-IS-NOTHING-WE-CANNOT-ACHIEVE!
~~~~~~~~~~~~~~~~~~~~~~~~~~~~

The hyphens will signify words that should be linked together with energy and intensity. The wavy line directs you to put tension into the phrase, to stretch the phrase as if it were a thick rubber band. Use a slash mark to represent a pause at the end of a phrase, a double slash mark at the end of each sentence.

- Warnings: "WE-ARE-IN-FOR-TROUBLE / IF-WE-CON-TINUE-TO-BORROW-TO-PAY-OUR-CITY'S-BILLS." / /

- Declarations: "WE-CAN-DO-IT / IF-WE-MAKE-UP-OUR-MINDS-TO-DO-IT." / /

- Accusations: "MY-WORTHY-OPPONENT-WAS-ABSENT / IN-THIRTY-TWO-OUT-OF-FORTY-FIVE-SESSIONS-OF-THE-HOUSE." / /

- Exhortations: "I-BEG-YOU-TO-CONTRIBUTE / TO-THIS-WORTHY-ORGANIZATION." / /

All should be marked as phrases to stretch and emphasize, with hyphens or with hyphens and underlining:

WE'RE THE LEADERS OF OUR CO.
& IT'S ABOUT TIME /
TO SHOW THE QUALITIES & ATTRIBUTES
WE'RE BEING PAID FOR. / /
I'LL DO SOMETHING ABOUT OUR ACT /
& U DO SOMETHING ABOUT YOURS. / /
WE MUST SHARE THE BLAME-&-THE-CREDIT /
THE BURDEN-&-THE-DELIGHT. / /

Remember, going down in pitch gives your voice a sound of greater authority. If you inflect up, you'll sound singsong and tentative. Mark your lectern script with arrows to remind you to go down in pitch at the ends of phrases and sentences, after questions, on adjectives, adverbs, and words before commas, and on anything you wish to emphasize.

A DESIRE FOR QUALITY IN LIFE↓

ARE U TIRED OF BEING TAKEN TO THE CLEANERS?↓

MONUMENTAL INDIFFERENCE↓

WE ARE GOING TO EXAMINE COSTS↓
                                        PROFITS↓
                                        TAXES↓
                                        MOTIVATION↓

To remind you to keep eye-sweeping throughout your talk and to deliver your opening and closing remarks totally eyes up, draw an eye symbol ◉ at the top of the first page, here and there in the margins, and at the conclusion of the speech. If you tend to have a stiff face, draw smile signs ‿ in the margins to remind you to animate.

REHEARSING, THE FIRST STAGE

When you have your lectern script prepared, you're ready to rehear(se) again. Rehearse aloud on your feet at least four times. The President of the United States may not be able to rehearse a speech four times, but I think you can.

In January 1980, I flew down to Washington on the eve of the President's State of the Union address. At eight o'clock, we met in the Treaty Room, a beautiful, awesome room, with Lincoln's conference table in the center and brocade walls covered with our country's most important treaties.

The President came in; he was wearing jeans. He had a copy of what was supposed to be the final draft, just finished because of the constant revisions. We went over the speech for an hour, shortening long sentences, marking for phrasing and coloring.

"Have you had suppuh?" he asked. I said I had. He went out

anyway and brought me back a beef and cheese sandwich, some peanuts and cheese snacks, and a bunch of grapes. He didn't want me to get hungry during what promised to be a long night. Then he left to have his own "suppuh." I went to work doing surgery on the sentences. I stayed at Lincoln's treaty table until after midnight —freezing. They really *did* conserve energy at the White House.

Compare your average day with a President's, and you'll see why you have no excuse for not rehearsing adequately.

President Carter rose at six to review the last draft (finished by a speechwriter at 5:30 A.M.). He had a breakfast meeting with a group of Evangelical ministers, a post-breakfast meeting with his staff, meetings with politicians and officials. Before he left for Justice William O. Douglas' funeral, he told Susan Clough to try not to let anyone make any more major revisions or changes in the speech. He returned at one-fifteen. What time did I want to rehearse, he asked. I said two. He said three. I said two-fifteen; he said two forty-five. We met at two-thirty in the family theater.

Only six pages of lectern script were ready. We began anyway. Each page arrived just in time for us to work on it.

There were constant interruptions, all of which the President received with grace and not a sign of irritation. His sense of humor never waned. He even skipped his daily jogging in order to have more time to rehearse. We finished at seven-forty; he was bleary-eyed and looked exhausted. He had just enough time to get dressed and be driven to the Capitol for his nine o'clock speech. But the rehearsal, even just two of them, paid off—no grin, body firm, better phrasing, more energy—the best-delivered speech he'd ever given.

As you rehearse, picture an audience in front of you. Tape each delivery and play it back, trying to listen objectively, as though to someone else. You don't have to cram-rehearse like a President. Space the rehearsal sessions a few days apart; do two or three run-throughs per session.

Rehearse the way actors do, *in-the-scene*, from entrance to exit. Walk resolutely up to the mock lectern. Your hands put the text on the lectern as your eyes are up, sweeping the room and saying, "Hello, I'm here, you lucky people." Take the stage, pause for a beat or two, and talk your opening two sentences without looking at your script.

Lectern Demeanor

As you rehearse, keep in mind some Don'ts:

DON'T lean on the lectern.

DON'T sway or shift from one foot to the other. Stand with your weight evenly balanced on the balls of both feet, body erect and steady, head high in Executive Posture.

DON'T fidget with your papers or rattle them (the microphone exaggerates noises). Dog-ear a lower corner of each page so that you can slide it easily to one side. There's no need to turn over a sheet, an eye-catching distraction. Even better is the speech-holder box we market that lets you slide each page into a well as you finish with it.

DON'T put your hands in your pockets or clasp them behind your neck or your back or fold your arms over your chest; in most cases those positions say "ill-at-ease" or make you look stern. Keep the index finger of your left hand moving down the margin. Keep your right hand still except when you're moving a page or (rarely) making a gesture. If the gesture is natural and spontaneous and doesn't distract, keep it. If it's choreographed, it will look phony. Words speak for themselves—you don't have to put up a finger when you say "one," two fingers when you say "two." I call that Mickey Mouseing. Watch your listeners' eyes. If they go to your hand instead of your face, you're being upstaged by your gestures. A good talk doesn't need gestures, and a bad talk never is made better by them. I don't teach gestures.

As you rehearse, picture skeptical faces in the audience. Speak with energy, momentum, enthusiasm. Keep contacting the audience in the mirror with your eyes, remembering to sweep the room like a horizontal windshield wiper, glancing down only briefly as you pick up the next phrase.

Forget the myth that looking at one friendly face will achieve warm communication with all; in actuality, that excludes and alienates everyone but the person you're focusing on. Imagine the room you're going to speak in—packed with faces. Constantly eye-sweeping all the eyes in a room gives action to your face. Sweep; don't dart from one side to the other. Speak a phrase to three or four listeners; then move your eyes to another group for the next phrase.

Start with the front row; eye-sweep, looking next toward the left middle of the audience, then at those farther back; sweep past the center middle, center back, right middle, right back. As you speak to your imaginary audience, think of those who'll be sitting way in the back. Act as though you'd make eye contact with them if you could. They will take your intention for the deed, and you will pull them into the radius of warmth you've created.

Your real audience will pick up your eye-sweeping rhythm and will develop a rhythm of listening expectation: your eyes are else-where momentarily, but the listener knows they'll soon be sweeping back to him. This rhythm holds listeners' attention. Also, always be eyes up on the words "I," "you," "we," "ours," "us," and on decla-rations, warnings, accusations, exhortations, recommendations, and questions, and on openings and closings.

Aim for "the ring of truth." Ask yourself, "Is this the way I sound when I'm talking to my friends about something we all care about?" Forget what you learned in a speech class, if you ever had one— don't elocute, don't recite. That will make you sound phony. "You can't convince if you don't speak with conviction," said Lyndon Johnson. If only he'd been able to speak to the nation that way, the way he spoke to his Senate buddies.

Record your speech each time you rehearse it and watch out on playback for anything that detracts from your delivery. Speak in the cadences of natural, spoken phrases. I once worked with the Prime Minister of a foreign country who, although he spoke no English, was on a good-will tour of the United States. I helped him write his speeches phonetically, and then I phrased them; he was able to deliver the talks in a conversational style. He called me as he was leaving for home. "I luff you, darlink," he said, "they thought I really could speak English."

Projecting energy from word to word within phrases requires the kind of concentrated physical force in your tone that you would bring to pushing a heavy piece of furniture. Keep the muscles of your vital triangle contracting to give intensity to your tone.

AIDING VISUAL AIDS

Most people love working with visuals. They feel less vulnerable sharing the spotlight. But visuals are only an adjunct to your talk or presentation. Use flip-charts, chalkboards, acetates, or slides only if there's no other way to make your points clearly, or if you're in a visual business, like advertising. Most visual aids are like lampposts drunks lean on—more for support than for light. They detract more often than they add. David Ogilvy calls them "vampire electronics."

Have variety in your visuals through color. White on black in a dark room is dull. Sometimes just a red-and-blue stripe across the top of an otherwise nondescript slide will give it life. Columns of figures can be referred to without a pointer if each is in a different color.

Type should be easily read from a distance of thirty feet. To check type size for visibility, hold your slides eight to twelve inches from your eyes. If you can't read them, the lettering is too small. Unless it's company policy, avoid reading exactly what is already on the screen. If you must, at least interject anecdotal information or additional evidence for relief.

Evaluate the lifespan of each slide. Some are complex and require study; if they leave the screen too soon, the audience is annoyed. Others have an immediate impact and are dead in three seconds; don't keep them on past audience interest. Begin and end with a strong visual.

Visuals need as much rehearsal as you do. Overlap the change of slides with conversation. Relate briefly to the screen and mostly to the audience. If someone else will work the projector, plan to rehearse with him beforehand. Be sure he understands your change-slide cues.

As you talk, keep your body turned toward the audience much of the time. Some speakers seem so fascinated by their slides they can't take their eyes off them. Almost the reverse should be the case. Except for a quick glance at the screen from time to time to check that the right slide is up, focus on the audience. The fact that they will be looking more at the screen than at you doesn't relieve you of the need to relate to them. Your audience will feel your presence even though their attention appears fastened on the screen.

If your speech requires a chalkboard or easel, do not display the information on it until the time comes to use it. That distracts. Peeling cards off an easel is easier and a great deal more graceful than setting them on. If you're using a chalkboard, write clearly so that your audience has no difficulty reading what's up there. Talk to your audience and maintain eye contact with them on your way to and from the board.

EVALUATING YOURSELF

At your third or fourth familiarization session, evaluate yourself. Acknowledge all those qualities in your delivery that we identified in the positive speakers; identify those less desirable qualities you'd be better off without, as well as those qualities you should work on.

Use this self-evaluation form to guide you in your rehearsing:

ACKNOWLEDGE	LOSE	ADD
attractive ———————	y'know ———————	———————
animated ———————	like ———————	———————
confident ———————	speed talk ———————	———————
conversational tone ——	slow talk ———————	———————
convincing ———————	chop talk ———————	———————
colorful ———————	high pitch ———————	———————
energetic ———————	nasality ———————	———————
enthusiastic ———————	shrillness ———————	———————
imaginative ———————	mumbling ———————	———————
interesting ———————	dullness, monotony ——	———————
good eye contact ——	lack of animation ——	———————
good voice quality ——	nervousness ———————	———————
good pacing ———————	fidgeting ———————	———————
good phrasing ———————	unnecessary details ——	———————
good pitch ———————		
good projection ——		
good bearing ———————		
credible ———————		

I'm often asked if there's such a thing as rehearsing too much. The answer is no—so long as you rehearse each time with commitment and energy and don't permit yourself to fall into dull rote memorization. Actors say it this way: "Give it the experience of the first time." Rehearsing—attitude as well as words—is much of the secret behind trading in the agony of nervousness for the ecstasy of holding an audience.

Your last rehearsal should be scheduled as close to delivery time as possible; otherwise the lectern script grows cold and doesn't feed itself up to you. Make sure you have a clean text—no cross-outs or corrections to distract you. Carry white-out or correction tape and a black felt-tip pen for last-minute changes.

Memorize opening and closing remarks so that you deliver them entirely eyes up. As you end your talk, "cadence out." That's an almost imperceptible slowing down, like a car before it comes to a full stop, a stretching out of the last few phrases that signals to the audience that you're concluding.

The four familiarization sessions should have weaned you from dependence on your text. You can scoop up a phrase or two in a single glance down now, perhaps a whole sentence. Your finger always moving down the left margin feeds the phrases up to you and gives you an enormous sense of security.

Being well-prepared takes away the one big reason for thinking negatively or wondering about how you'll do. Now you're ready for the remaining steps that will help you banish stage fright forever.

5

Bye-bye Butterflies, Hello Confidence

Replay in your mind a stressful situation—an important job interview, a presentation to clients, talking to the president of your company. Recall your signs of discomfort as you realized that others were seeing a substandard version of you. Your normally steady hands trembled; your voice was a quivery, high-pitched version of itself; your words didn't say what you meant them to say. Some idiot was babbling, and that idiot seemed to be you. The culprit was nerves.

There are two kinds of nervousness. Positive nervousness, racehorse nervousness, an almost trembling eagerness to be off and running—that's productive. The adrenaline flows, the brain is acute, the reflexes quick, the eyes bright. That kind of intense excitement adds luster to your presentation.

Negative nervousness paralyzes. It's the knot in the pit of your stomach, the sinking feeling. It makes your palms sweat, your throat and lips dry. It freezes your face, gives your eyes a look of panic, makes your heart feel as though it will burst. Negative nervousness dulls the responses and perceptions, numbs the judgment, turns the body into an awkward, inept betrayer. It creates the overwhelming urge to run away. It's a protector when you're crossing a street and see a truck coming at you; it's a killer when you face a room full of people. Negative nervousness robs you of authority, effectiveness, and poise when you need them most.

When I ask people what they think causes their nervousness, almost the same explanations turn up on everyone's list: being unprepared; feeling inadequate, stupid, unattractive, or uninteresting; having nothing to say.

But one fear covers all the rest like an umbrella—the fear of looking ridiculous to others. What you fear is humiliation, not being perceived by others as you'd like to be perceived.

The good news is that, through a combination of physical and mental controls, nervousness can be prevented.

PHYSICAL CONTROL OF NERVOUSNESS

I started to put the formula together when I was playing the role of Lady Thiang, the Queen of Siam, in *The King and I*. Yul Brynner had a nightly backstage ritual. Just before the opening curtain, he would stand in the wings and plant himself an arm's length away from the brick wall, place his palms on the wall and lunge against it with such force that the veins of his shaved head bulged.

I asked him why on earth he was doing that. Through clenched teeth he replied, "It keeps me from getting nervous." So I tried it. There we stood, the King and Queen of Siam, dressed in gold and silk, pushing fiercely on a wall.

Something astonishing happened. The sick tremor of stage fright that always accompanied the sound of the overture didn't happen. I realized that the muscle tension kept it away.

The triangle of muscles that physically control nervousness are the same ones that support your voice. To remind yourself, reread Chapter 2. Here are three ways to find out how the muscles of your vital triangle should contract to control nervousness:

1. *The Teakettle* (Chapter 2).

2. *The Siamese Dancer.* Stand with legs slightly apart, weight balanced evenly on the balls of your feet, palms together at breast level, with elbows raised so that your arms are parallel to the floor. Take a small sip of breath through your mouth and, as you exhale

with the sound of a long shshshsh, press the heels of your hands together with all of your strength, at the same time contracting the
muscles of your vital triangle.

3. *The Balloon.* Make a tight fist and pretend it's a balloon that
is half inflated. It takes enormous effort to inflate fully. Put your
fist to your mouth and blow with all the pressure you can muster.
With your other hand, feel the muscles of your vital triangle contracting. Do you feel them pulling B-A-A-C-K, B-A-A-C-K,
B-A-A-C-K?

The muscles of your vital triangle control nervousness because
the solar plexus, one of the major nerve-control centers of your
body, lies behind that triangle. It affects the production of adrenaline—the chemical that galvanizes you for action with positive
nervousness. But the solar plexus also can produce noradrenaline
or norepinephrine, the chemical that makes you panic.

Contracting the vital triangle muscles reduces or stops the production of norepinephrine. Controlling the process aborts almost
any negative emotion—not only fear and anxiety, but also anger
and pain and depression—any emotion that might get the better
of you. You can use these emotional brakes when you're in the
dentist's chair, when you're lining up a twenty-foot putt, when
you're tired or feeling low.

Control of the solar plexus also anesthetizes you against the cold
(try briskly walking a short block on a single exhalation). For a
pick-me-up that's better than a martini, draw yourself a tub of cold
water, take a small breath and pop in. Then count to sixty on a
single exhalation, take another breath and jump out. If you have
the nerve to try that, you'll find you're not shivering afterward, but
tingling and invigorated. (Again, this trick is not for you if you
have even a hint of a heart problem.)

Contracting your vital triangle energizes. If you're climbing a
flight of steps, climb as far as you can on a single exhalation. You
won't reach the next floor exhausted and out of breath. My husband and I do this on the golf course when we're approaching a tee
at the top of a sharp rise. We get to the top breathing normally.

The side benefits of contraction on exhalation go on and on. It
works like magic in preventing nausea, because pulling in the muscles inhibits reverse peristalsis, which results from motion sickness.

Try tightening your vital triangle the next time a plane you're in encounters some turbulence.

You can contract your vital triangle muscles anytime, anywhere. You can do it while you're asking for a raise, while you're waiting to give a talk, while you're chatting with some VIPs at a party, while you're appearing before a Senate investigating committee. Whenever you do it, you can be in control of your nervousness.

If you put that contraction together with one other little trick, you'll be a lot more than simply not nervous.

MENTAL CONTROL OF NERVOUSNESS

Spinoza theorized that expressing an emotion on one's face created that feeling within; thus, rage is accelerated by its expression, and so is joy. You may remember the song "Put On a Happy Face." Happy faces have a boomerang effect. When you radiate happiness, people are inclined to smile back, which makes them feel even better. When you project confidence and joy, you change the atmosphere around you just as surely as one sour person pulls down the mood of an office or a dinner party.

Can you project positively if you feel low? Actors learn how to convey silent messages by saying to themselves over and over the words that convey a mood or feeling. We call that "motivating." They concentrate on a thought so intently that the audience gets a message or feels a mood. In the last act of *The King and I,* when, with no lines to speak, I had to express sorrow, I was able to create tears every night by concentrating intently on sad thoughts. The tears got me a Hollywood contract.

You can project joy, friendliness, and empathy by concentrating on four phrases that give out positive vibes. Every time I teach the following technique to sophisticated executives, I preface it with a mock apology. "It may sound like hokum," I say, "but it's hokum that works." My clients try it and it works. It's never regarded as silly.

The first two phrases, "I'm glad I'm here, I'm glad you're here," communicate joy and ease. The third, "I care about you," projects concern. "I know that I know" gives the message of authority.

Study the diagram:

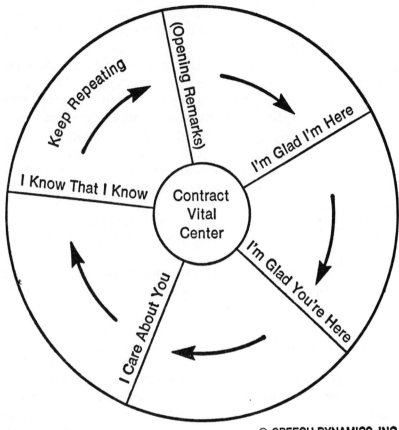

© SPEECH DYNAMICS, INC.

Put the wheel like a record on the turntable of your mind and play it as you repeat the phrases nonstop, over and over. Make yourself feel what you're saying. This tactic works in the same magical way that singing a cheerful song gives your spirits a lift.

Repeat the phrases until you can say them automatically non-stop like a chant. Say the entire litany two or three times in one breath. Forcing yourself to say the phrases nonstop and fast revs up your body, generates positive energy, and gives you intensity.

Now combine contracting your vital triangle muscles with a repetition—first out loud, then silently—of the phrase wheel. The combination of the repetition of the phrases and the contraction of the vital triangle muscles keeps you too busy to wonder about how you're going to come across to others. That timing wheel generates positive vibes, presence, and power. It helps you resist any inclination to think negatively.

The final ingredient in the formula to control nervousness is one last return to anticipation. Never approach anything that matters to you without putting yourself through an intense and imaginative cataloging of possibilities. What is the most likely negative scenario? After you've imagined yourself going through it, rewrite the script several different ways. If your competitor or worst enemy is seated in the front row, how do you keep in control of yourself, and of him? If your time suddenly is cut to ten minutes, how will you get in what you have to say?

Anticipate. Adapt. Be flexible. A few minutes of good-natured ad-libbing is better than repeating prepared material that someone else beat you to.

Preparing the talk is "Get ready"; rehearsing it is "On your mark." "Getting set" is getting everything ready before you leave the starting gate to win the race.

THE DELIVERY ROOM

Go to the room where you'll be speaking long before the audience is due. Chairs arranged in straight rows make for a chilly atmosphere; it's worth taking the trouble to have the chairs rearranged in curved rows. People can see one another's reactions; the Greeks knew what they were doing when they designed the amphitheater. Have the first rows of chairs as close as possible to the platform; that adds intimacy and increases the sensation of the audience that it's being spoken with, rather than at. You can seem to have a sold-out house if you have fewer seats available than the number of people expected. Fold up chairs if you have to, and stack them at the sides of the room. Or rope off sections at the back if the chairs are stationary and fill up the front part of the room.

Check all the equipment. See that you have enough light on your text. Beware: Lectern lights often illuminate Adam's apples and double chins better than they do pages. You can tape a blank sheet of paper over the light to diffuse the glare. Check the height of the lectern itself. You'll look ungainly if you tower over it, dwarfed if it's too high for you. Ideally, a lectern's top should reach to about the bottom of your ribcage. If the lectern can't be adjusted, try to find a riser of some kind to place under it or under you. At one seminar I participated in, Gianni Agnelli, the head of Fiat, was charmingly introduced by Clare Boothe Luce. Mr. Agnelli crossed the stage to Mrs. Luce, kissed her gallantly, and acknowledged her introduction. Then he got behind the lectern and all we could see of him for the whole of his speech was his head bobbing up and down behind the lectern, like a cork in the ocean.

Place your text as high on the lectern as possible, so that your eyes will have the shortest possible distance to travel from text to audience. If the papers slide downward because of a steep pitch, a book or ruler along the bottom ledge will position the text higher.

If you're using visuals during your talk, ask to have the room as light as it can be without sacrificing sharp definition on the screen. People get sleepy if a room is dark. The person controlling the lights should have a script with cue marks for speeding the dimming and brightening of the room.

Ask for the sound engineer so that you can test the microphone. The sound engineer can adjust the volume to the right level for you and the tone control to flatter your voice. (If your voice is high-pitched, ask to have the control moved toward "bass.") Feel free during the course of your talk to call out to the sound engineer (it will help if you've learned his name) if the volume is too loud or if people are having difficulty hearing you. He also is there to help you out by turning up the air conditioning if you notice people fanning themselves or nodding.

Try out the microphone. Position yourself about eight inches from it, closer if your voice is soft or if you want a warm, intimate sound, farther away if you tend to boom. Draw back a few inches when you deliver forceful phrases; if you pop your "p's" or hit your "t's" too hard, speak into the microphone at an oblique angle. If the microphone squeals or screeches, you may be touching it—some mikes, like some dogs and babies, don't like to be touched. In general, familiarize yourself with the equipment so that you can adjust it smoothly if a previous speaker had it in a position good for him, bad for you.

If you must drink, limit yourself to one drink. Eat lightly, so that you won't feel sluggish.

Study the audience while others are speaking. Do they respond quickly? Slowly? Negatively? Do they laugh easily? Is their attitude what you expected? You may want to amend a statement, modify an argument, add a joke or omit one. (Unless you're fully confident, though, don't make a last-minute change in the basic structure of your speech.) Look as though you're listening to the other speakers. It is a courtesy that the audience will like you for. You also may hear something you'll want to react to in your own speech.

Make sure your notes are in order. I've seen inexperienced speakers lose their place and panic.

Unless they're part of your public image, or unless you're nearly blind without them, don't wear your glasses. If you must wear them, put them on just after you've delivered your opening remarks.

When Tracy Austin beat Chris Evert Lloyd in the U. S. Open and became the youngest tennis player to win the women's championship, she was asked how it felt to be the youngest champion ever. Tracy smiled broadly. "I didn't think about being the youngest," she answered. "I just thought about the champion part." While you're waiting to go on, keep Attitude Adjusting. Spin the wheel nonstop in your mind: your opening sentences plus, "I'm glad I'm here, I'm glad you're here, I care about you, I know that I know." And keep your vital triangle contracting:

> "Good afternoon. A wise man once declared that if you would civilize a man you should begin with his grandmother, I'm glad I'm here, I'm glad you're here . . ." And again and again until you're introduced. (The wise man, by the way, was Victor Hugo.)

If you keep repeating the phrases and your opening lines nonstop, your mind works for you, not against you. You're revving yourself up with energy, enthusiasm, and confidence. Sit upright— sagging in your chair costs you body intensity and the look of presence. Also, you're not able to control the muscles of your vital triangle in that position. Keep contracting your vital triangle as you exhale slowly, letting the air leak out through your lower teeth.

YOU'RE ON!

Walk to the lectern smartly. Project joy, authority, and confidence. You have no reason not to—you're thoroughly familiar with your text and your delivery. If you seem to be at ease, your audience will be at ease. They'll reflect your attitude and your face. They came wanting to like you.

Audiences are remarkably supportive. I once saw audience empathy at work during an international convention, when a vice-president, a shy man given to sitting at meetings with his head over his doodles, got up to speak. He stood paralyzed at the lectern, completely mute, turning red and shuffling through his text as though he couldn't find his place. As we sat there feeling his pain, he lifted his head and, with a gallant attempt at humor, said weakly, "I should have consulted with Dorothy Sarnoff before I tried this."

I jumped to my feet. "It's not too late," I cried. I hurried up the aisle and put my arms around his middle. That took audience attention off him, and I could feel his relief. "The most important thing for you to know," I said to him, "is that we love you, right?" The audience roared approval.

I squeezed the man's waist to put a vise around the muscles of his vital triangle. I told him firmly, "Now, contract these muscles; tighten them like a girdle as hard as you can. Are you doing it?"

He nodded, a look of hope on his face. "All right, go!" I said, and returned to my seat. He picked up his report, read it without hesitation in a normal tone of voice, and was thunderously applauded.

You'll never need that kind of help because your hours of intelligent anticipation, preparation, and diligent rehearsal are about to pay off. You know what you're going to say, and you know how you're going to say it.

When you reach the lectern, put your notes as high as possible on it. For a beat or two, eye-sweep the audience; let your eyes communicate, "I'm glad I'm here, I'm glad you're here . . ." Animate your face. Radiate joy. Stand chest up, stomach in, weight evenly distributed on the balls of both feet. Feel your presence and power. You are in control of yourself and the audience.

Your eyes and animated face make the first electrical connection with them. Don't just look at people; look into their eyes. Their eyes will keep their ears receiving.

As you speak, keep your antennae up. If you see disconcerted eyes, you may be speaking too fast or too slow. Adjust. If eyes seem to flinch, the microphone may be too loud; move away from it. If you see eyes watching your hands, you may be gesturing too much.

Listen to audience sounds and silences; they tell a lot. Restless moving in seats, whispering, coughing may mean you're not energized enough and you're losing them.

After the first act of a performance of *The King and I,* Yul Brynner complained to Oscar Hammerstein that the audience was dull. "Never blame the audience," Oscar said. Yul went back out after the intermission and energized his performance, and the audience responded in kind.

Check your watch now and then to make sure you're keeping on schedule. Have passages in mind that you can drop without loss if you're running over. Give your last remarks, like your first ones, totally eyes up. After your final word, hold your listeners' eyes for another beat and murmur a quiet "Thank you."

HANDLING HECKLERS

It's exceedingly rare for a speaker to be interrupted by a heckler, even when the subject is controversial. Interruptions do, however, occur occasionally, especially at stockholders' meetings. If you have a heckler, beam benevolently at him. Handle him with care and courtesy and you keep the audience on your side. Put him down and it may cost you audience empathy. Look the heckler straight in the eye when you answer and lean toward him slightly. That focuses audience attention on him and may make him freeze. Offer the heckler a chance to talk during the question and answer period if you're having one, or assure him that you'll answer his remarks when you've finished your talk. If you act in control and look at him with a benevolent face, the audience will help you take care of him.

QUESTIONS AND ANSWERS

To protect a question and answer period, have three or four questions planted in the audience. While you're answering those questions, others will be gathering courage to ask questions of their own. If a lull does set in, fill it by putting forward questions yourself: "The other day someone asked me . . ." "People often wonder whether . . ."

Keep your replies brief, repeating a question only if you think the audience hasn't heard it or understood it. If a question is too long or is simply a cover-up for a speech by the questioner, cut it off with tact, quickly summarizing the question he seems to be asking.

If you don't know the answer to a question, say so. I once saw a political candidate destroy an otherwise forceful appearance during a question and answer period. What did he think, a reporter wanted to know, of the recent appointment of Thomas Watson as ambassador to Russia. The candidate looked puzzled for a moment. Then he smiled and replied, "Why I think Senator Watson will learn as he goes along." The audience gasped. Thomas Watson was chairman of IBM.

Don't be tempted to allow the question and answer period to run on too long. When you feel you've hit a peak and before interest wanes, bring the session cordially to a close and thank the audience warmly for their attention.

PLANNING A LARGE MEETING

I plan and design many large meetings and conferences for corporations. A primary consideration is the ambience of the room, which depends to a large degree on the arrangement of the furniture. The usual long, straight table for panelists stretching across the front of the room is one I avoid, as I do putting the speaker's lectern off, way off, to one side. The speaker sees the panelists, with whom he may have to interact, mostly in profile, and sometimes the panelist at the far end not at all. The panelists can't see one another either, unless they bob their heads and shift their chairs.

The ideal arrangement for a panel of speakers has the lectern at the center, with tables for the panelists on either side of it. Angle the tables like elbows, so that the panelists can see one another and can interact with eye language. Again, whatever the form or size of your meeting, the atmosphere will be more conducive to communication if the chairs for the audience are arranged in curves rather than straight rows, and as close to the platform as possible. The warmest, most responsive group is one in which people can see one another.

Explain in advance to the convention center or hotel how you want the room arranged for your meeting; send a diagram along with your other requirements. If your program includes a panel discussion, order enough microphones—it slows things down if the panelists have to pass the mike around or jump up and down to get to the lectern. Green plants on a platform warm up a meeting environment. Front spotlighting on the participants lets the audience see their eyes. Avoid cold fluorescent overhead lighting; that never flatters anyone, least of all women—makeup turns a ghastly shade. If you must have fluorescents, request warm fluorescents, rather than the regulation ice-blue tubes.

While we are on the subject of light, consider, while you're planning the program, how visual effects will be integrated. Don't overdo the trendy, disco, overbusy light and sound effects and multiscreen slides that have become so popular lately. The recent epidemic of visuals and special effects upstages speakers. At a convention in New Orleans, the president of the company insisted on speaking with nothing on stage but a plain backdrop. Following the thunder and lightning of the rest of the program, his speech was a tremendous relief—a person after all that noise. Meetings can be entertaining as well as informative, but they shouldn't rival a Las Vegas floor show.

Planning the participants is even more important than planning the setting. Start and end with your strongest speakers. Contact every speaker at least two weeks before the event and ask what subject he plans to cover and what his main points will be. Try to avoid overlaps, gaps, and crossed wires. Intelligent planning and checking protect speakers from echoing one another's material. Tell each speaker his time limit when you first contact him. In subsequent checking ask if he has worked on the speech. If he tells you he hasn't started it yet, pleasantly establish a time a few days hence when you can recheck with him. In the end, he will be grateful.

If You Are Chairing

Prepare your opening remarks as conscientiously as you would a full-length speech. The first three or four minutes of a meeting establish its tone. Also prepare your summary in advance. You can tuck in extras as the participants speak and provide new thoughts for you. Both opening and closing remarks should be delivered eyes up—remember, that requires rehearsal.

Get to the meeting place on the scheduled day before the audience arrives. Be there early enough to check seating and sound system. (See the suggestions for speakers in the last section.) Generally, it's best to keep the light in an auditorium at about one half to three quarters of full brightness—warm light improves the creative response; darkness makes people sleepy. Check the temperature of the room. Too warm a room makes everyone sluggish; a chilly room—under 65° F.—makes people want to get to someplace warmer. (Not necessarily always a bad idea; one company keeps the room a frigid 60° F. during its stockholders' meetings and finds that cuts down on the attendance and participation of noisy and disgruntled stockholders. Another company solves that problem by inviting the dissidents to lunch before the meeting, serving them a few drinks to defuse them and to find out what's on their minds. If you expect hostile stockholders, consider scheduling your meetings at about two-thirty, or as late in the day as you can get away with; meetings are apt to be shorter when people have to leave to get home.)

My favorite story about scheduling meetings concerns Tallulah Bankhead. The two of us were serving together on an actors' board, and the chairman suggested a Monday as the date for the next meeting. Tallulah, who was known to imbibe a bit over the weekends, rejected that with a fluttering of eyelashes. "Oh, dahlings," she said, "never on Monday. Monday is my sinus day."

Assemble your participants before the meeting. Tell them the order in which they will speak and also that you mean business about time limits. Establish the signal you'll use to let them know time is almost up; it could be pointing to your watch or discreetly tapping on a glass. (At one celebrity banquet, twenty people invited to pay tribute to the guest of honor were given one minute each. At the end of that time, they were warned, the spotlight would be shifted to the next speaker. It worked.) Have your own schedule neatly typed with the beginning and ending times of each segment noted in the margin in red, like a timetable.

To start the program, tap firmly on the microphone with your finger. Tap with authority—once, twice, three times. Don't scold if people don't fall silent instantly; people do like to finish their sentences. If you're having trouble getting quiet, scratching a fingernail on the mike makes an abrasive sound that brings instant attention.

With as much energy in your body as you have when you're serving at tennis, say a warm "Good morning!" and make your brief welcome. If there are people to thank, give a blanket acknowledgment if possible: "Our thanks to all who have worked so hard to make this meeting a success." If individual acknowledgments are required, ask the audience to hold its applause to the end. Introduce dignitaries on a dais with dispatch: "Since time is short and we want a full opportunity to hear our speakers, I'm going to introduce the distinguished people at the head table nonstop. Please hold your applause until they've all been presented." Say each person's name as though it were the most important in the world. To him it is. And identify each person with a colorful adjective or phrase. (At one luncheon, the wife of the president of Smith Barney concluded her introduction of the C.E.O. of Merrill Lynch by noting that he was the only person she knew who had given up smoking ten minutes after he said he would.)

Reinforce the request to hold applause by the rhythm of your introductions. If you pause for a beat between one name and the next, the audience will think they should applaud after all. Your pacing, tone, energy, and drive must say, "This is an express—no local stops."

Major speakers require more than a sentence or two, but only returning heroes merit more than a minute (about 170 written words). Half that time generally is enough—so long as you get it right. I remember a banquet at the Waldorf-Astoria many years ago, when Grover Whelan, New York City's official greeter, introduced David Dubinsky, head of the International Ladies Garment Workers Union. Whelan launched into a lengthy and extravagantly laudatory introduction and then, just as he should have said "David Dubinsky!", stopped dead and looked horrified and turned to the speaker. "What's your name again?" he asked in despair.

If your program includes a series of speakers, acknowledge each person's contribution briefly as he finishes and make a transition to the next speaker. "Thank you, Jane Fowler, for helping us understand some of the complexities of operating the Museum of Man and the heroic struggle of your group to raise funds. Our next speaker, James Owen, has a different approach, since he can tell us where our exhibits come from . . ."

If your program is a panel discussion, ask the panelists to come prepared with questions for their colleagues but not to interrupt until all the expositions have been given. Ignite the subsequent discussion by engaging two participants: "Jim Owen, your comments seem to suggest that Jane Fowler's group has an impossible task if it hopes to present a comprehensive display. What do you two feel about that?" Cut the panel discussion time off before interest wanes, when it's still at its peak.

If your program includes an audience question and answer period, explain the ground rules. Request that questions be brief: "In that way, we'll be able to hear from as many of you as possible." Question and answer periods, as I've noted, need stage managing in order to make them go smoothly. At one seminar in which I participated, Henry Kissinger and John Connally were on a panel together. Most of the questions were directed to Kissinger, and Connally almost faded from sight. If one or two of your speakers are getting the lion's share, redirect a few questions to the neglected panelists or ask one of an excluded speaker yourself, or ask him to comment on another panelist's answer.

A minute before the time for the question and answer period is up, announce that you'll take only one or two more questions. Stick to that, and end on time.

Deliver your prefabbed and fleshed-out summary, thank the speakers, thank the audience. Be brief: "You've been a wonderful audience. We look forward to seeing you next year."

If you've followed the suggestions above, your audience will look forward to seeing you again too.

If you run large meetings with any frequency, you will probably find it useful to have attendees complete a speaker or convention evaluation form. These forms, which can rate hotel facilities, workshops, and social activities as well as the individual speakers, provide program planners with valuable feedback. A sample of such a form follows:

SPEAKER NAME _____DAY OR DATE_____

A. Please rate the speaker's:

1. Speaking ability

Skilled in presenting material, voice and presence excellent	_____1
Adequate, does not detract from session	_____2
Poor speaker, detracts from session	_____3
Poor speaking techniques, a serious handicap to learning	_____4

2. Ability to explain

Explanations extremely clear and to the point	_____1
Adequate explanations	_____2
Inadequate explanations	_____3
Explanations seldom given even when asked	_____4
Question not applicable	_____5

3. Knowledge of subject

Exceedingly well informed in field	_____1
Adequately informed	_____2
Not well informed	_____3

4. Attitude toward participants

Enthusiastic, very helpful and concerned	_____1
Moderately helpful and interested	_____2
Routine in attitude—little individual contact	_____3
Distant, aloof, cold, little interest	_____4

5. Attempt to involve participants

Highly encourages and values involvement	_____1
Values, but does not actively encourage involvement	_____2
Seems indifferent to involving others	_____3
Discourages involvement	_____4

6. Value as a tool to help you learn

Highly valuable	_____1
Good value	_____2
Somewhat useful	_____3
Valueless	_____4

7. Did the speaker appropriately assume your level of prior knowledge?

Right on target _____1
Generally correct _____2
A bit inappropriate _____3
Inappropriate _____4

As an alternative speaker and/or follow-up session I would recommend:

_____

_____

TITLE OF SESSION _____

B. Please rate this session's:

1. Organization

Systematic and thoroughly organized _____1
Adequate, could be better _____2
Lack of organization, detracts from session _____3
Confusing and unsystematic presentation _____4

2. Level of content

Beginner _____1
Beginner and intermediate _____2
Intermediate and advanced _____3
Advanced _____4

3. Potential audience

Of general interest to most members and spouses _____1
Of general interest to most members only _____2
Of general interest to most spouses only _____3
Of interest to a small number of members and/or spouses _____4

4. Content

Extremely relevant and up to the minute _____1
Relevant _____2
Somewhat out of date _____3
Basically "old hat" _____4

5. Stimulation of new ideas

Extremely stimulating _____1
Stimulating _____2
Not much stimulation _____3

6. Fulfillment of your expectations

Received more than I expected   _____1
Received what I expected   _____2
Received less than I expected   _____3
Other_____

7. Take-home value

Extremely useful and directly applicable   _____1
No immediate application, but generally useful   _____2
Neither applicable nor useful   _____3
Other_____

The effectiveness of this session could be improved if:

6

Positioning Yourself to Get the Job You Want

I had just finished a session with the C.E.O. of an automobile company, and I opened the door to my next appointment. He was sprawled on a black lounge chair. All I saw was a huge paunch. Then I took in the rest—a sloppy-looking, sad-faced, young middle-aged man. The details filled themselves in: two tiny sad eyes encased in fat, a mouth that was a slit, a turkey neck from chin to collar line.

He tiptoed into my TV studio. His wife had told him to call me for an appointment, he said. He had been head of a video communications group for a large corporation. Two years ago the accounts he supervised had resigned, and for six months he had just sat at his desk reading magazines until the company let him go. For a year he free-lanced. Now a head hunter had sent him out on several interviews. Nothing.

Howard told me he'd been in analysis for six years and had just found his confidence. I asked him to write down the questions a prospective employer could ask that would make him uncomfortable. The questions he wrote down were the usual ones: Why did you leave your last job? How much money are you looking for?

We role-played an interview. He handled my questions clumsily and haltingly, obviously ill at ease as he lolled there, his paunch

like a mound of quivering Jell-O. If I had played him back after
that taping, it would have destroyed him. I wanted to be constructive, to show him he could present himself in a different, positive way.

On the second take he sat forward in his chair in alert, vital executive posture, his jacket buttoned. He looked tidier, thinner,
more assertive. I asked him to talk to me with his eyes and face
and to work for momentum, to finish each phrase, not stop every
minute or two to gather his thoughts.

Then I played both versions back to Howard and asked him to
look at the man on the screen through the eyes of an interviewer.
"I wouldn't hire him," he said after version one. "He looks fat and
lazy and sloppy—and timid and scared." The man in version two
was "more like someone I'd hire."

It took us two more sessions—and red stickers for Howard's
watch and refrigerator that put him on a serious diet—to make
both of us view the final tape with genuine enthusiasm.

THE FIRST IMPRESSION

An executive recruiting firm, Business Careers, has isolated six
main reasons why 234 unsuccessful candidates for sixteen corporate presidencies didn't get the jobs they were after. Herbert T.
Mines, president of the recruiting firm, says that the six reasons
seem also to explain why candidates fail to get high-level jobs
below the presidential level. The reasons:

• Inability to project a special competence in interviews.
• Frequent job moves without marked advancement in salary or
responsibility.
• Failure to project objectivity, or appearing to be emotional and
subjective.
• Lack of clarity in expressing views.
• Overcriticism of former employers.
• Poor appearance, dress, or grooming.

Although some of the reasons may seem minor, says Mr. Mines,
it may be important for job candidates not to give even the
slightest reason for rejection. One candidate was rejected, he says,
simply because his costly vested suit made him appear overweight.

Above a certain level of salary and responsibility, the job interview is called a position interview; above the level of the position interview, the job interview is called meeting for lunch. In the theater it's known as an audition. Whatever it's called, at some point in all of our lives, we are judged for something we want very much. For many people, a job interview is more stressful than a TV interview. There may be a lot more riding on it.

Most of us have little idea of how to present ourselves to advantage. We cross our fingers and hope the interviewer will like us, that our qualifications will do the selling job for us, that no better applicant turns up.

Ann was typical. "People tell me I don't seem very sure of myself," she whispered breathily. She had failed in every job interview. Ann was twenty-five, an M.B.A. magna cum laude, and— when she took off her huge black-rimmed spectacles and stopped rolling her eyes each time she answered a question—quite attractive.

We went to work. In her first video playback she saw herself as others saw her—eyes rolling and downcast, face pinched with anxiety, clothes mannishly severe. By the time we had finished, Ann had presence, carried herself with authority, wore a chic suit, perched her glasses on top of her curly hair, animated her face, and projected in a firm, melodious voice. She combined beauty, brains, and talent.

Jerry was brilliant, frustrated by being told by interviewers that the opening required someone with less impressive credentials. He was aggressive and heavy-handed. When we played back our role-playing interview, he saw it immediately. "I'm not overqualified," he said. "I'm overobnoxious." Jerry had to retailor his self-presentation.

When they learned how to maximize themselves for an interview, both Ann and Jerry ended up with top positions. Ann became the vice-president of a large investment house and sent me her boss, the president, for a client.

PREPARATION

First you sell yourself, then you sell your skill, commodity, or idea. You may have exceptional expertise, innovative ideas, superb skills, but if your personal presentation leaves something to be desired, you may not realize your full potential.

When you've managed to land an interview for a job you want, it's anticipation and preparation time. Research the job and the company as thoroughly as possible. Business libraries and reference libraries are a source of information about corporations and industry trends. Browse through Standard & Poor's news reports and executive registers, the Moody's manuals and the Value Line Investment Service, to learn about the company's services, growth patterns, and competition. Your stock broker may have additional information.

People in the company or in the same line of work are a useful source. Find out from them about management's style—are the employees generally content? does the company help people advance? which departments provide the best opportunities for promotion? Researching a company can help you decide whether or not you want to work for it; it also helps you to impress an interviewer with your interest and with your intelligent approach to a situation.

Of the fourteen factors that were found by another study to lead to rejection of a job applicant, seven are interview-related. Chief among the pitfalls found in a survey conducted by Northwestern University of 186 companies is the inability to demonstrate self-confidence, enthusiasm, and a clear set of goals. Although there is no such thing as a typical job interview, personnel experts agree that there is common ground and that most questions are designed to find out more about you than the dry data they appear to elicit.

Questions fall into several categories:

• WORK EXPERIENCE: Questions about your previous jobs are an attempt to get beneath your résumé. Why did you leave your last job—always the most difficult question of all to answer. Don't express bitterness about a former employer—it speaks ill of your discretion. What are your career goals? Sometimes an interviewer will ask bluntly what they are; more often that's the question behind "Why does this job interest you?" You may be asked what you like doing best and what you like doing least, and whether or not you enjoy being part of a team effort. The interviewer is looking for evidence of adaptability, competence, motivation, leadership, ability to deal with others.

An interviewer may ask you about your strengths and weaknesses. Adapt your answers to the job you're seeking. If you're after a job in sales, stress your persuasiveness; if you're up for a position as a magazine editor, you may want to talk about your ability to come up with ideas.

Talking about your weaknesses should be merely another opportunity to show your strengths. "I have a tendency toward perfectionism," sounds like an admission of weakness, but it's something most employers welcome. "I tend to be a bit of a workaholic" is another. Employers love workaholics.

•EDUCATION: Straightforward questions about your best and worst subjects, how you financed your education, your extracurricular activities are an attempt to learn about your feelings regarding authority, your ability to acquire knowledge, your versatility and qualities of leadership.

•FAMILY AND EARLY YEARS: Questions about family are designed to explore how much responsibility you're shouldering and how well you're managing it. Sometimes interviewers who ask casually about your childhood—the town where you grew up, your family structure—are not making small talk. By inquiring about the stability of your childhood, they believe they can discern your self-image, your degree of motivation and emotional and social adjustment.

•PRESENT ACTIVITIES AND INTERESTS: Questions about your hobbies and spare time give interviewers added insight into your judgment, your breadth of interests, your social skills. These days, employers look favorably on those who engage in some (but not too many) outside professional, political, and volunteer activities, particularly if they dovetail nicely with the field of work.

Typical questions:
   •How was your last employer as a person to work for?
   •What would you rather have done more of in your last job?
   •What aspects of your last job did you like least?
   •If you could have made one suggestion to management in your last job, what would it have been?
   •Would you tell me about the best boss you ever had? About your worst boss?
   •What is the hardest thing you've ever done?
   •If you could live your life over again, what changes would you make?

• What qualities do you think this company should look for in a person filling this position?

• Would you tell me how you spent your spare time last week?

• What do you think is likely to make the difference between success and failure in this position?

• Would you tell me about your health in recent years?

• What do you feel has been your greatest accomplishment in life?

• What has been your greatest disappointment?

• As an employee, what can management do to assist you in functioning effectively?

• What have you done in the past year to improve yourself?

• How does your spouse feel about your taking this job?

• If you are hired, how do you see your future with this company?

• What do you consider to be your greatest strengths and your greatest weaknesses?

• What are your pet peeves, the things that upset you most?

• How does this position compare with others you are considering?

• What are your own criteria for your success?

• What do people most often criticize you for?

• What do you most often criticize others for?

• What factors in your past have contributed most to your development?

• What factors would you say have been handicaps in preventing you from moving ahead more quickly?

• What else do you think I should know about your qualifications?

• What else would you like to tell me about yourself?

One of my chairman clients favors this question: What is your "Walter Mitty"? That's a version of what I'm told is the "in" question this year: "If you weren't you, who would you most like to be?" Winston Churchill answered that best years ago, though at a dinner party, not at a job interview. "If I couldn't be who I am," he replied, "I would most like to be Lady Churchill's second husband."

Touchy questions. Laws have been passed prohibiting employers from asking female applicants questions about marital status, family planning, and the like, which they don't also ask of male applicants. But many employers continue to ask those questions. You have every right not to answer (and indeed to report the company to the Equal Employment Opportunity Commission), but the result may be only a state of unemployed self-righteousness. If you do choose to answer such questions (or even to volunteer the answers unasked), a straightforward statement that your children are cared for by a housekeeper, for example, or that your divorce is in the distant past, will answer the questions asked and the questions underlying them as well.

Money—specifically how much you're currently earning and how much you'd like to make in this job—is the most difficult subject. About your present salary, many personnel experts recommend judicious truth-stretching. If you do fib, it's highly unlikely you'll be found out. Virtually no personnel department will release salary information to a prospective employer. (To find out your own company's policy, call your personnel department posing as an employer calling about a former employee.) And if you're interviewing while still employed, the interviewer probably won't even bother to call at all to check if you tell him your current employer isn't aware of your job search. It's important for you to know the top of the salary range for the position for which you're applying. "What do you expect to pay for this position?" is the sort of question with which to counter a query about money. A cool "It falls in that range" is the best answer if you're able to elicit a number from the interviewer.

Role-play

To prepare yourself properly for a job interview, rehearse, role-play. For that, you need a friend and a tape recorder. Give your friend the list of questions above, or one that you've devised. Begin as you would in a real interview with an opening remark. Comment on the splendid view, on the friendliness of the staff, on a recent merger or a newly announced product. Ease in talking about yourself the way you'd talk about a product can make the difference in getting an offer. One client of mine, during an interviewing for a magazine writing job, said that he flew his own small plane. He suggested that he easily could fly himself to hard-to-get stories. He landed the job.

Have your role-playing interviewer ask questions first as an empathetic interviewer, then as the cold and haughty kind who tries to shake you up. Have him ask you innocuous questions about college and then pitch you a curve like, "Do you live with someone?" Try to anticipate personal questions you would prefer not to be asked. Get set now with a choice of answers that will make you appear composed later in the real interview.

Your tape recorder can help you in your practice sessions. Do you sound knowledgeable and assured? Do you answer questions concisely, or do you ramble? Have you managed to put across your strengths and your suitability for the job?

Have a choice of closing remarks ready. Practice establishing a date with the interviewer on which you can expect to hear from him or when you may call him.

If an interviewer hits a nerve, that can be your undoing. Have you ever had a drinking problem? A nervous breakdown? Do you have a criminal record? Were you a draft dodger? Very often it's your attitude toward a problem rather than the problem itself that tips the scale. "I'll bet I'm the first person you ever interviewed who spends time on a kidney dialysis machine," smiled one applicant for a vice-presidency early in his interview. He disarmed what could have been a problem question and wound up with the job. A painful truth is best brought out into the open, and initiated by you. But only you can know whether it will cost you more to reveal an apparent handicap than to worry about keeping it hidden. If you choose to be open, try several different answers and rehearse carefully what you will say. Consider whether you can cast the revelation in a positive light, as something that adds dimension to you. Look your interviewer in the eye throughout even if he looks away.

THE REAL THING

The common wisdom—and advice with which I concur—is to dress in conformity with the employees in the office where you hope to work. Decide what to wear a few days in advance. That way, you won't be thrown off balance on the big day by an unexpected spot or tear or unshined shoes.

Be on time. Allow extra travel time, plus fifteen minutes. Being late is always a very big minus—it makes a bad impression; it makes you nervous. You're flustered with apologies instead of calmly prepared when you greet your interviewer. It's also the easiest minus to avoid. If the company is large, allow extra time to find the right office.

Check with the receptionist for the pronunciation of the interviewer's name if you're unsure. While you wait, have an opening remark on the tip of your tongue. Attitude Adjust, revolving the positive phrases on the turntable of your mind and contracting your vital triangle on exhalation.

Make an entrance! Walk into the room animated, energetic, head up, chest high. Being pleasant-to-be-with is written by implication into every job description. You never get a second chance to make a first impression.

Look the interviewer in the eye and shake hands firmly. A wet-fish grip makes a negative impression. Go for an upright chair; if you have no choice, resist lounging in an overstuffed chair or sofa. Sit in executive posture, only the lower part of your spine against the back of the seat.

Remember that fidgeting, ear-pulling, leg-swinging are distracting and that you can control your tension by pressing your thumbnail hard into the palm of your other hand. Be eye-to-eye 90 percent of the time.

Non-edited talkers cost a company too much time and money. At the same time, monosyllabic replies make you seem inarticulate. Avoid hard luck stories, apologies, and recitals of past illnesses—don't leave negatives for the interviewer to remember you by. Listen thoughtfully, and ask pertinent questions of your own in a nonprovocative manner.

When you feel that the questioning is drawing to a close, end the interview yourself. That demonstrates that you value time and have a feeling for the structure of a meeting. Shake hands smiling, thank the interviewer, and depart with dispatch—don't ooze out.

If some or all of your interview takes place over lunch, a few additional words are in order. I once visited the painter André Brasilier at his château in France. Brasilier proudly showed off his dining room, noting the tall fourteenth-century mirror over the buffet. "You know," he said, "the French rarely had mirrors at seated eye-level in their dining rooms. They considered the face never uglier than in the act of chewing."

The French had a point. When you're attending an "eating meeting," where food and talk share the table, avoid "chew" foods. Choose soft foods: fish, quiche Lorraine, omelettes, ice cream. Choose neat foods. Avoid soups, they slurp; salads, they slop; spaghetti, it spots. And speaking of chewing, gum is out.

RÉSUMÉS

Before, during, or after your interview, you'll need a résumé. Most likely before, since in most cases a résumé precedes a face-to-face meeting. Numerous books are available on how to identify your skills and sell yourself on paper, and a trip to your library should net you some helpful material. There are, however, a few hints that you may not find in those books.

1. If you're sending out a fusillade of résumés to companies where you have no contact, a covering letter—individually typed and addressed to a specific person, not to a "Sir" or "Madam"—increases the chances that your résumé won't land in the circular file and will even get you an interview. Some experts suggest that you address your letter and résumé to the president of the company even if you're after an entry-level job. Such letters normally are passed on to Personnel or to the appropriate department, but they may get special handling there. Whoever gets your résumé for action never knows whether the president just might follow up on it, especially if your presentation is impressive.

2. Like speeches, covering letters and résumés inform and communicate; they should have the elements of a persuasive speech. Many of the rules that apply to writing a talk apply to résumé and cover-letter writing. Research the company carefully so that you can state with precision in your covering letter what you can do for the company. Don't use jargon—the personnel director may not understand it; the fifty-five-year-old vice-president may be put off when he realizes how out of touch he's become with developments in his field. And there's always a chance that some résumé reader is fond enough of the English language to toss your résumé in the wastebasket because of an overabundance of jargon.

Keep your sentences short, your words simple, your verbs active. Even if you have a Ph.D. in English, have someone check your letter and résumé for spelling, grammar, typographical errors, and clumsy or repetitious expression.

3. Always ask for an interview in your covering letter, but don't use that word if you can help it. Instead, ask when you might come in for a brief meeting. Write as though you expect that meeting to occur. Indicate when you'll be in the town if it's not your own. Follow up with a telephone call to arrange a suitable time.

4. Avoid designating in your résumé or letter a specific job title. A more general designation, e.g., Personnel Management, rather than Personnel Manager, will permit you to be considered for a wider variety of openings.

5. There's no need to tell your race, of course, but if you're a minority group member and think that fact will increase your chances, it's more effective to indicate your status by listing the organizations to which you belong than by stating your status alongside the condition of your health and your age.

6. Speaking of age, you may want to omit that statistic if you're over fifty-five. If you're between forty-five and fifty-five, though, make sure you include it. Otherwise, people may think you're older than you are. Whatever your age, show it in date-of-birth fashion. If you don't, a passing birthday may make your résumé obsolete.

7. Don't state an expected salary range or your present or prior salary on your résumé. That discussion is for the interview; you can't negotiate with a piece of paper. Listing your salary range or salary may lose you jobs for which you easily could qualify or make you appear overqualified.

8. If your physical dimensions (height and weight) stated in print conjure up a picture of a well-put-together human being, by all means include them. Also include them when they line up with the direct physical requirements of the job you want, say, if you're after a job as a jockey. Otherwise, leave out that data.

9. The same is true for your marital status and the number of children you do or don't have if you're a woman and you think there's some sexism at the companies to which you're applying. You may be better off leaving out that information and dealing with it during your interview.

10. Unless you're given to missing large chunks of work time because of your health, list your health as excellent. Like the labels on cans of olives describing their size, adjectives nowadays mean a lot less than they're supposed to. If you can't say your health is excellent, say nothing.

11. Whether you prepare your résumé in the standard chronological form or the more unusual skills-listing style, leave no time gaps. Don't let a potential employer think you spent two years in jail or a mental institution or sailing around Tahiti. You can be brief, or you can embroider, but do account for all of your time.

12. Unless you really cannot write and organize a résumé, it may be better to avoid the résumé-writing services, especially if you're applying to large organizations. Those services do very professional-looking work, but by now their standard language and format have been seen so many times by large employers that they're often ignored.

If you do choose a résumé-preparation service or a career counselor of any kind, do some comparison shopping first and try to get a personal recommendation. At a minimum, check with the Better Business Bureau or local business-licensing agencies to see if there have been many complaints. This is an area that attracts charlatans.

13. Reproducing your résumé on good, clean paper is appropriate if you're not yet at a supervisory level. If your immediate or long-range aim is higher, have your résumé reproduced by multilith or photo-offset on good-quality paper (twenty-pound weight, 50 percent rag content at a minimum). Have the résumé printed on only one side of the sheet.

Some experts suggest that printing your résumé on buff or light blue paper will make yours stand out from the hundreds of others an employer receives. That may be so, but stay with white if you're applying for a job in finance or law, if you're looking for work outside a major metropolitan area, or if the companies to which you're applying are the least bit conservative. The same advice holds for the typeface in which your résumé is typed or printed. In no event use a script typeface.

If you're attractive and if appearance has some relevance to the job requirements, you may want to include a picture (printed on the résumé itself, not attached). But omit a picture if the companies to which you're applying are in the white-paper-résumé category.

The fine line between a distinctive résumé and one that elicits a "not our kind" response from prospective employers is a hard one to draw. If your qualifications are strong and if you're suited for the job for which you're applying, your best bet may be to play it safe. That goes for the form of your résumé as well as the style, using a standard chronological recital of your employment rather than the less common format in which you list your skills. The less likely you are to be considered for a job, the more reason there is to try to distinguish yourself in some fashion—whether by printing on different-colored paper or running a decorative border along the top of the page or writing a humorous opening paragraph in your covering letter. When your chances are slim, you haven't all that much to lose, and you may as well let some distinguishing characteristic help you stand out.

If you're unsure about using a "creative" résumé, send several first to companies you don't care very much about working for and see what kind of response you elicit. If it's good, send the résumé to companies you'd like to work for.

14. Remember that everybody is a prospective employer, or knows one. Give copies to your friends, relatives, hairdresser, butcher, broker, and candlestick maker. You never know.

WHEN YOU'RE THE INTERVIEWER

Your responsibility as interviewer is the obverse of the interviewee's. Empathize and try your best to appear interested, even if this is the hundredth person you've seen today. Be cordial; don't deep-freeze the applicant and make him sweat to thaw you out.

Learn in advance as much as you can about an applicant, through letters, application forms, and telephone inquiries. The interview should be only the fleshing out.

While you're interviewing, have the courtesy to pay full attention; don't take phone calls, rearrange papers, glance through correspondence, or otherwise indicate that the interview isn't important enough to have your undivided attention. Try to put the applicant at ease. Start with a casual remark or two; ask about his college career or summer jobs if he's a recent graduate, his field of work if he's not.

Don't rehash the vital statistics of an applicant's résumé or the static facts of his career. Get a feel for his attitude toward his work, his family, hobbies, background. Assess his personality. The questions listed earlier in this chapter can serve as a guide.

Avoid questions that elicit only yes or no answers. You'll get little information. And don't put an interviewee into an artificial stress situation as some experts recommend. The way a person handles that kind of "pressure" is no indication of how he'll perform on the job.

Ask some self-appraisal questions: what he learned from being a scout leader, what prompted him to move to a new city. If you keep asking "how" and "why," you'll learn a great deal. Hold back on exploring for negative aspects until late in the interview.

Clarify as well as you can the nature of the job for which the applicant is being considered. The other part of your job as an interviewer is to sell your company to promising candidates. Ask the applicant what he wants to know about your company or the job and tell him just that.

If you feel you need time to decide, tell him. Leave him cordially, even if you don't plan to employ him, but don't be so overwhelmingly cordial that he thinks he has the job when he hasn't. After the interview, try to make your decision while facts and impressions are fresh in your mind.

7

The Work Scene

Communicate and Motivate
Subordinate Diplomacy
Women and the Sound of Assertiveness
Redesigning Yourself for Strength
Rating Yourself
Maximizing Office Meetings
Work Stress

Henry Kissinger, it's said, knew how to get the best work out of his staff. Each time an aide came tremblingly to his desk with a report, Kissinger fixed him with a piercing gaze and asked, "Is this the best you can do?" The aide would hesitate, back out, and return the next day with an improved version. Kissinger would glower menacingly and ask again, "Is that the very best you can do?" Away would go the cowed aide. On the third day he would return, proffer the report and announce, "This is the very best I can do." "All right," Kissinger would say. "Now I'll read it."

How to get others to work productively for you and how to do your own best work have been popular subjects of company and personal concern. Having your message givers send the messages about you that you want received, recognizing the value of anticipation and preparation, knowing the tricks of controlling nervousness, and projecting a positive image add up to making you a person with presence. And that's the managerial style you should aim for.

What you should not have is a style that I blame for the number of young executives I've seen crippled by feelings of inadequacy, loss of self-confidence, action paralysis, and even nervous tics. A recent article in *Fortune* magazine on the Twelve Toughest Bosses summed up that particular behavior in the words of one of them: "Leadership is demonstrated when the ability to inflict pain is confirmed."

The twelve toughest bosses all shared one harrowing characteristic, said their staffs: they inspired awe, respect, and often downright fear. Since those men head major corporations, there must be some benefit to their style. But in the end, intimidation is costly. Few people can do their best work in a threatening, anxiety-creating atmosphere. The majority react with resentment and sometimes active or passive sabotage.

"How do you spot a leader?" asks Robert Townsend. His answer: "They come in all ages, shapes, and conditions. Some are poor administrators, some are not overly bright. One clue: the true leader can be recognized because somehow his people consistently turn in superior performances."

Of the thousands of presidents and chairmen of the board with whom I've worked, those who get the greatest productivity from their employees are those who treat the people who work for them with concern, decency, and fairness. Those men and women are what I call "lovingly assertive"—a combination of being understanding and intelligently constructive. They inspire a spirit of cooperation. They believe in what is known in management jargon as Theory Y, which makes the following assumptions about employees:

1. That expending physical and mental effort at work is as natural as expending the same effort at leisure.

2. That people can and will exercise self-direction and self-control to attain objectives to which they're committed.

3. That rewards and the satisfaction of achievement commit employees to attaining company goals.

4. That most people want to accept and seek responsibility.

5. That most people are capable of exercising ingenuity, imagination, and creativity in solving organizational problems.

6. That in modern business life, the intellectual potentials of most employees are under-utilized.

Effective executives know how to set realistic goals for their staffs. They understand the power of motivation and the power of encouragement. In one insurance company, the staff was divided into three groups—high, average, and low achievement. The officially labeled high-achieving group surpassed even its superior performance; the middle group also improved dramatically, as a reaction to being labeled mediocre. The group labeled a failure did indeed fail, dropping substantially in productivity.

COMMUNICATE AND MOTIVATE

In one of the early episodes of "All in the Family," Archie complained to the parish priest that his Italian neighbors were taking Edith to so many functions at the local Catholic church, they must be trying to convert her. "If Edith seems interested," said the priest, "maybe that should be telling you something. Why don't you try to communicate with her?"

"Why should I try to communicate with her?" Archie growled. "We live in the same house."

A manager communicates even when he doesn't think he's communicating. When, like a petulant spouse, a manager says nothing, becomes cold and uncommunicative, goes into an "office sulk," he's signaling that he's displeased with a subordinate, perhaps that he thinks the subordinate is hopeless. The silent treatment communicates the manager's own inadequacy in dealing with a problem. He doesn't know how to look at a situation in the way a doctor analyzes a physical malfunction, diagnoses it, and prescribes treatment for it. It's crucial to the success of your office that you be able to communicate with your staff with strength and tact. An indifferent or abusive approach leads to poor performance by everyone.

It's important to listen, to what's not being said as well as to what is being said. Take Jerry, a supervisor, who's listening to one of his staff:

> Well, Jerry, I finally locked up the X Company order. Boy, was it a mess! But you said it was an emergency job, and I saw to it that it went out today—right on the button. You know, I've been here every night this week and almost all last weekend to tie that darned thing up. X's specifications are ridiculous, but the order's on its way, even though my wife may throw me out. And let me tell you, if I never see another job as tough as that one, I'll be plenty happy.

If Jerry answers, "Great, Joe. Now let's get to work on the Y

Company order," he really hasn't been listening. It's hard to know what Joe really was saying, but he wasn't saying simply that the X Company order was difficult. Probably he was asking Jerry for a pat on the back. Man's greatest need on this planet is for survival; his second greatest need is for approval. Frequently in offices people manage merely to survive.

Hostility

Anger is rarely a useful tactic for getting what you need. The director of my first Broadway show was the legendary Max Reinhardt. He was a great teacher and a sheer delight. In one scene, in which I had to swirl around in a Viennese waltz, the train on my gown was too long, and I tripped on it during the first rehearsal. I asked that it be fixed. At the next rehearsal, the problem remained, and at the next and the next. At the final rehearsal, I tripped on the train again. I raised my arms over my head and shouted, "Stop!" In the hush that followed I stalked to the footlights and declared furiously, "Unless you shorten this hem at once, I'm not going on with the rehearsal."

Instantly someone from wardrobe appeared. Reinhardt came over to me and murmured in his soft voice, "Bravo! But remember: only use temper when there is no other way to get the job done."

Aristotle put it this way: "Anybody can become angry—that is easy; but to be angry with the right person, and to the right degree, and at the right time, and for the right purpose, and in the right way—that is not within everybody's power and is not easy."

Angry bosses rarely get the best work from their staff, but neither do professional nice guys. The best way to motivate employees is by offering them earned recognition, achievement, growth, responsibility, advancement, and satisfaction in the work itself. The employer who depends on personal loyalty often causes discomfort and resentment. Loyalty and responsibility to the company are what should be developed. Nice-guy employers often short-change their employees. Refraining from interfering with a subordinate in order to develop his initiative and skills is constructive and commendable; refraining from interfering just to avoid trouble often brings on worse trouble.

One client was sent to me ostensibly for help in making speeches. "While you're at it," said his boss to me, "see if you can't do something about his manner. He's a good man, but he brutal- izes people, and that's creating problems."

The vice-president turned out to be an uncomfortable man with a buttoned-up, hard-eyed face. We began by videotaping his speech; his delivery was stiff and monotonous. To find his natural conversational tone, I asked Arthur about his work; when he spoke about his staff, it was with a trace of contempt. Yet he clearly ad- mired his boss, a man supportive and interested in his employees.

I discussed the principles of loving assertiveness with Arthur. "If I let up on my people," he protested, "they won't toe the line."

"I'm not suggesting that you compromise your standards," I said. "You carry a lot of responsibility, and your department has to function well. But you could have so much happier people and get so much better results."

We role-played his most recent encounter, with a junior execu- tive whose report was late. When he saw his video playback, Arthur acknowledged that his style wasn't the kind that made peo- ple want to deliver for him.

We switched roles. Using what I call the inverse approach, I discussed the problem, exploring and understanding rather than condemning. I asked Arthur, now the subordinate, what had hap- pened to delay the report. "You usually do such good work," I said. "What happened?"

Arthur explained that he had had too many projects due at once.

"What do you suggest we do in the future so that this doesn't happen again?" I asked pleasantly.

"Call for help," Arthur offered.

"Good idea," I congratulated him. "Let's try it that way. Next time get Joe to give you a hand. It causes too much trouble for all of us when a report is late."

We watched the playback, and Arthur gave it grudging ap- proval. "It seems the long way around to deal with it, but I see your point."

I showed Arthur how to put a brake on his temper. Whenever he felt about to explode, he could defuse his hostility by consciously controlling the muscles of his vital triangle and have time to choose his words carefully and undamagingly.

Arthur's boss called to thank me. "He's a new man," he marveled. "The whole atmosphere has changed in his department."

Alternative Approaches

Arthur wasn't a new man, he had simply chosen an alternative and better behavior. He talked some months later to one of his subordinates about his altered attitude. "Well, you see, sir," said the employee, "we have kind of noticed it, but we just don't believe it. We're waiting for you to change back. Somehow we were more comfortable the other way. We could blame an awful lot on you."

Alternative behavior is always available. One textile company executive had two juniors on her staff who were causing her problems. The first was extremely competent but consistently overstepped his authority, causing difficulties for Phyllis and for her department. When we role-played she saw that she was not taking the time to clarify her instructions when she assigned a project. She had a talk with her assistant later in which she complimented him on his initiative but made it clear that he would have to moderate his enthusiasm. Phyllis decided to include her subordinate in decision-making meetings and found that once he had a better understanding of underlying objectives, he was able to see where his authority ended and hers began. He became a more productive member of her team, and she was able to accomplish that without causing resentment.

Phyllis' other problem subordinate wasn't so easy to set straight. Marcia blamed Phyllis when she missed a deadline, resented her work, which represented a demotion from her previous job, was obstructive in every possible way. Phyllis reiterated Marcia's responsibilities, clarified her deadlines, insisted she be told in advance if Marcia anticipated having trouble in meeting them. But after several months of trying every means of motivation, Phyllis finally had to admit that Marcia stood like a roadblock in the progress of her department. She told the personnel director, "I just don't think I should be spending time teaching someone how to behave." Marcia was transferred.

Sometimes the lovingly assertive alternative involves cutting your losses. There's no way really to explain office chemistry. It's better if you have what I call "matching metabolisms." A fast-moving boss needs a fast-thinking secretary; a sluggish person can irritate and hold back a whole team. You have to know when you're so at odds with someone who's working for you that it's a kindness to him as well as to you and to the company to replace him.

SUBORDINATE DIPLOMACY

The lovingly assertive alternative works just as well when you're in the subordinate position. One television producer role-played a confrontation with her boss who, she said, frustrated her at every turn.

I played the part of her boss. With eyes flashing, she declared: "It's absolutely essential that we use dancers on the Brazil show. I've been over this with you time and again. It makes the show fall flat without them. I need your approval on the budget right away."

"I'm hammering at him," she exclaimed on seeing the playback. "Why would he say yes? I'm a shrew."

We discussed alternatives. She could express her concern that the show lacked color and ask his advice. She could suggest, in a pleasantly businesslike way, "Could we cut the budget for special effects so that we could include the dancers?" Her manner could be pleasant and warm. In the battle of the office, talent is the punch, tact is the fancy footwork. The inverse approach is tact.

Getting What's Coming to You

Often the cast of characters in an office includes too many tyrants and too many patsies. The patsies fear confrontation; they cave in with an apologetic smile even when they're right. Patsies don't make enemies, they make ulcers, for themselves and for others.

The meek do not inherit the earth. So if you're nonassertive, why not change your presence, your approach, and your rewards. Alison was an investment counselor with a Philadelphia firm and so outstandingly able she wrote the firm's daily market analysis. Her salary had not been raised in years.

"What happens when you ask for a raise?" I asked.

"They turn me down."

When Alison role-played a scene in which she asked for a raise, it turned out that she just hinted. She chattered about the high rate of inflation, how much she'd like to go on a cruise, the new car another executive was driving.

We tried a different tack. First Alison announced her objective. Then she made her points and discussed her present options. She finished by stating what she wanted. Her script went roughly like this: "I'm here to discuss my salary with you. When I joined the firm seven years ago, I was paid twenty thousand dollars a year. Since then you've given me added responsibilities. The daily market analysis goes to twenty thousand subscribers now, and it brings this firm a good deal of business; it's quoted in newspapers, which helps our business and our prestige. I'm asked to address seminars and give interviews, all of which I do on my own time. I've become enormously more valuable to this firm in those seven years, and my salary's risen only ten percent in all that time. I've done some research on what my current value is in the marketplace; three firms in New York have offered me over thirty thousand dollars. But I'd rather stay in this city with you."

Alison, well-rehearsed, got her raise, and something else for which she had hungered—respect.

WOMEN AND THE SOUND OF ASSERTIVENESS

Women in business often complain that they have a hard time winning respect. Sometimes that's because they lack assertiveness, they lack presence, they seem tentative. To an extent, that shows up in the way women express themselves. Linguist Robin Lakoff has suggested that because their social roles are so different, men's and women's speech patterns are almost different enough to be regarded as different dialects. According to Lakoff, women's language—language used typically though not exclusively by women —has these characteristics:

1. Use of "empty" adjectives, e.g., "divine," "lovely," that do not have connotations of power.

2. Frequent use of modifiers or hedges, e.g., "sort of," "kind of," "I guess."

3. Use of a questioning intonation at the end of a declarative statement, which gives their voices a singsong quality, as well as more frequent use of tag questions, e.g., "don't you think?"

4. Extensive use of "so" with an adjective, as in "so many people."

5. Use of hypercorrect grammar and excessively polite speech.

These characteristics, says Lakoff, make women's language expressive and polite, rather than direct and informative. It is definitely nonassertive.

Psychologists Faye Crosby and Linda Nyquist of Boston University tried an experiment using Lakoff's findings. They studied conversations at a police station between police personnel and their clients; most of the clients were there to make an inquiry. Crosby and Nyquist found that the clients, both male and female, used "women's language" more than either male or female police personnel. They suggest that "women's language" is used by people in roles that tend to lack power.

Women seem to have a harder time than men with confrontation, but confrontation isn't easy for men either, especially in an office setting. Consider, even write down, the things about your job you'd like to change. What have you tried to do about them? What have been the results? Start devising scenarios for what to do and say the next time you're faced with a problem. Then evaluate the reaction you think you'll get, and if necessary revise or develop alternatives. Role-play with a friend, first playing the intimidator yourself so that your friend can get an idea of how to play him or her. Tape your role-playing session and listen to yourself objectively. Did that person hold his own?

REDESIGNING YOURSELF FOR STRENGTH

Once at a dinner in Hollywood, Charlie Chaplin entertained the guests throughout the evening by imitating people they knew—men, women, and children, his chauffeur, his servants, his secretaries. Finally he sang at the top of his voice an aria from an Italian opera—sang it superbly. "Why, Charlie, I never knew you could sing so beautifully," someone exclaimed. "I can't sing at all," rejoined Chaplin. "I was only imitating Caruso."

If you want to present a more assertive image, play a little game with yourself. Stand in front of a full-length mirror and pretend you're the person who dominates you. Imitate the tone of voice, the bearing and mannerisms, the expression in the eyes and on the face.

See how strong and confident you feel when you're playing that person. You can use the trick by play-acting—walking into a meeting pretending you're Margaret Thatcher, or the chairman of the board. Take those same characteristics and incorporate them into another person—yourself.

Adopt them to make yourself more forceful. Nonassertive people often miss opportunities to show themselves to their best advantage. Bob suffered a setback when he was transferred to a department where his new boss, an arch-rival of his old boss, froze him out. Bob became timid. We decided he would prepare himself to make a first-rate contribution at every meeting. At every session he put something worth thinking about on the table and soon earned everyone's respect, including his own.

Project yourself strongly by taking time to think up ideas or a new approach or by doing more than what's expected of you. Aim to leave a little of yourself behind when you exit.

BOSS: I want you to pull out material so we can start planning next season's campaign.

YOU: I've been thinking about the market analysis that came out last week. There's a slight trend toward noneffervescent drinks that I think is significant. People really are switching. My hunch is there's a big future in drinks like iced tea. It doesn't have the additives some other beverages do. That's an attractive plus, and . . .

Your attitude toward yourself and others is remarkably effective in controlling situations. I once had to lecture to a club audience known among lecturers as the "terrifying torturers," a nightmare collection of wooden faces, nonreactors, fidgeters. I studied them as I waited in the wings to go on: "Show me" was written on their faces. I declared silently: "You people are going to look so much better when I'm finished with you."

I bounded up to the lectern and shook them up with energy and enthusiasm. Within ten minutes they looked alive and happy and a lot younger. The vitality I projected created vitality in them, and I was rewarded with hearty applause at the end.

At almost every moment you probably have more alternatives than you realize; controlling your attitude toward yourself and your work affects others' attitude toward you. Phillip was a guitar-playing college kid for years after college until he ran out of money and joined his father's dress-manufacturing business. He loathed his job, which was selling to department store buyers. His mother, a former client, asked if I could do anything to help—her husband was about to throw her son out.

I asked Phillip to pretend I was a buyer and to sell me some dresses. He was indifferent and unenthusiastic as he thrust each imaginary dress at me. He didn't have to say that he hated selling dresses; it certainly showed. "Think of it this way," I said. "Every time you extend your arm with a dress in front of you, don't think of selling the dress. Think of it as taking care of your future." That took the resentment out of his attitude. He went on to enjoy what he was doing and eventually to become the head of the company.

You can select your attitude just as you select your tie or your dress in the morning. Focus on the positive aspects of your job—it's experience you'll use sooner or later, one way or another; it's a stepping-stone to something better; at the very least, it buys dinner and pays the rent.

RATING YOURSELF

Whatever your position in business, you're constantly being evaluated. What you may not be aware of are the qualities for which you're being judged. The following chart, a Performance Appraisal from one major corporation, sets out the categories. Use it to grade yourself and to see where you need improvement:

	UNUSUALLY STRONG	GOOD	NEEDS DEVELOP- MENT	UNSATIS- FACTORY
1. Supervises department well on a day-to-day basis:				
a) Organizes workload; sets priorities and meets time-tables.	——	——	——	——
b) Responds with a sense of urgency; good follow-through.	——	——	——	——

	UNUSUALLY STRONG	GOOD	NEEDS DEVELOP- MENT	UNSATIS- FACTORY
c) No ongoing strategic problems.	——	——	——	——
2. Develops people:				
a) Ensures that everyone has a development plan.	——	——	——	——
b) Allows people to function independently.	——	——	——	——
3. Client relationships:				
a) Understands the business, the market and its problems.	——	——	——	——
b) Sets a tone of partnership.	——	——	——	——
c) Focuses attention on big issues.	——	——	——	——
d) Listens well.	——	——	——	——
e) Forges effective personal relationships.	——	——	——	——
4. Leadership:				
a) Uses research resources to develop sound strategies.	——	——	——	——
b) Clearly communicates issues and objectives to people.	——	——	——	——
c) Has presence.	——	——	——	——
d) Uses research data and judgment.	——	——	——	——
5. Business growth:				
a) Initiates and develops business building programs that are strategically sound.	——	——	——	——
b) Contributes to clients' plans. Helps set program priorities.	——	——	——	——

Whatever you may think of evaluation forms—and experts disagree about their value to a company—they are becoming widely used.

MAXIMIZING OFFICE MEETINGS

According to one recent study of managerial work time by Professor Henry Mintzberg of McGill University, executives spend an average of 69 percent of their work life in meetings of one sort or another. In another survey, published in 1979 by Alec MacKenzie and Associates, executives ranked meetings as the fourth-biggest time-waster—the first three were time on the telephone, drop-in visitors, and ineffective delegation. Ross Barzelay, president of General Foods and one of my favorite clients, says he knows he's hired the wrong person when he's asked to attend too many lower-echelon meetings.

Herbert Meyer reports in *Fortune* that executives generally agree that "the core problem with meetings is not so much the amount of time they absorb as the amount of time they waste. More precisely, executives agree that what screws up so many meetings is everybody else's inability to perform effectively and efficiently before an audience." In brief, suggests Mr. Meyer, what's needed to run a successful meeting is an ability to choose the right participants, to guide them briskly through the business at hand, and then to send them back to work. In France the leader of a meeting is called an *animateur;* his job is to give life to a meeting or conference.

Meeting Time-savers

A clear strategy for decision-making meetings can save you and your company time and money. Jim Kerley, executive vice-president of Monsanto, requires each staff member to bring to a meeting a memorandum of no more than two pages stating: 1) the subject he wishes to present; 2) the issue within the subject; 3) information about the issue; 4) a personal recommendation (this section may take up no more than three inches on the typed page); 5) a conclusion.

Begin before the meeting by sending each participant an agenda defining the subject or object of the meeting, reviewing (briefly) the current status of the problem. State the length of the meeting, who will be there, and how long you expect each person to talk.

Try to hold the number of participants at a decision-making meeting to no more than fifteen (doubling up—including the head of a department and his second-in-command—is a common barrier to efficient decisions). The representative should have the authority to make decisions for his department; decision-making meetings can't succeed if their members don't have decision-making authority. If you must have a larger group—more than twenty-five—break it into smaller units of six or so. Have each unit examine the problem separately and come to a decision. Each unit then sends a representative to a final meeting group, with the others involved listening in as audience.

The Seating at Your Meeting

An oval or round table lets all eyes see all other eyes, and the chairperson can be aware of who is confused, irritated, approving, or out to lunch. If you have the usual rectangular conference table, however, the best place to sit is at a corner, since you can see all faces from there. The more eyes you can read and send messages to, the better you can control the meeting.

When you begin the meeting, tell the participants how long you intend it to last. And start on time—this is probably the most frequently violated of all rules for effective meetings. Don't wait for late arrivals; consider the people who came on time.

Meeting Momentum

A meeting should have momentum. If it's well-planned, you can get through a great deal in a short time. Overlong meetings are usually caused by lack of discipline on the part of the chairman. If you are chairing, look like a leader. Meeting-room chairs often are enemies of authority and alertness. If you loll back in a half-horizontal lounging position, you look too casual. An upright body makes you look more alert and gives you more presence. It makes for energized communicating. Clicking and twirling pens, fidgeting, untwisting paper clips, picking on nails are viewer distractors. Even if the speaker isn't looking at you, give him the courtesy of your full attention. When you talk, look into the eyes of each person in turn, leaving out no one. Even if the subject is serious, you can be animated.

Gauge how you're doing by monitoring others' eyes and body

language. Bored people doodle or look apathetic. When the meeting's pace slows, so does the group's thinking. You are the *animateur,* the ringmaster; move the meeting along with energy and dispatch.

As others speak, jot down points they suggest on which you want to comment. I'm often asked about how to abort the long-winded speaker. Observe his breathing rhythm as he talks. Feel the timing. Anticipate when he is about to take a breath, and slip in with a statement.

Listening

Don't be too quick, however, to cut others off. There may be potential there. Having respect for all opinions makes for productive and constructive meetings. Ideas that could have been rejected as visionary often are transformed into practicality. Evaluate. Ask yourself: Why did the person who made the suggestion think it was worth proposing? Is there anything of value in his idea that you can acknowledge, even though you may reject it?

Suppose you say, "Tom, you seem to be suggesting these two processes would work better if they could be combined into a single operation. I'd never thought of that way of approaching the problem. It might lead to some very interesting possibilities." Build from there. Doing that doesn't commit you irrevocably to the suggestion, but it does show that you're receptive, and it puts everyone at the meeting in the right frame of mind for making the best of that idea.

What do you do if an idea has been worked on conscientiously and constructively by the group and still doesn't seem strong enough for adoption? Try another version of the Kissinger "Is that the best you can do?" approach. The best course for continuing harmony is to set the idea aside for the time being, not to reject it with finality. Suggest that the idea has uses that may help solve another problem later. That way you save face for the person who suggested it. You also may prevent a feeling of letdown among the others who have given their best efforts. And possibly, the idea may be helpful at a later stage.

Encourage profitable discussion and hear out disagreement. As an old professor said to a new instructor, "I can't give you any theoretical advice on pedagogy, but I'll tell you one thing from experience. It will frequently happen when you are holding forth that some boy in the class will disagree. He probably will shake his head violently. You will be tempted to go after him then and there. Don't do it. He probably is the only one who is listening."

WORK STRESS

Clients who come to my office from their own often come straight from stress situations. That shows in the way they talk, the way they carry themselves, the way they describe their objectives. Stress is not just another word for nervousness. Nervousness is acute and usually related to a specific situation—delivering a presentation, going on a television show, tackling some sticky personal problem. Stress generally is a more chronic state. We all experience a certain amount of stress. Like positive nervousness, a reasonable amount of stress can be productive. Sometimes, however, the level of stress rises too high for comfort. The test below, devised by psychologist Frances Merritt Stern, director of the Institute for Behavioral Awareness in Springfield, New Jersey, is designed to help you evaluate your on-the-job stress level.

To score, write 1 (for the least), 2, or 3 (for the most) for each of the following statements. In deciding which number to use, consider how intensely you experience the discomfort and how often the situation arises. An intense stressor that occurs often, for example, would rate a 3. A stressor that occurs rarely and/or is not very intense would be rated a 1.

1. I lose sleep over work-related problems.

2. I think I'm worth more than my paycheck shows.

3. I dread being evaluated by a superior or boss.

4. I worry about dealing with deadlines that can't be met.

5. I'm afraid others' expectations of me in my present job are unclear.

6. It's difficult for me to criticize another's work.

7. I don't feel good about myself because of my job.

8. It's frustrating not being part of the decision-making that alters the scope of my job.

9. My back and/or neck tense while I'm working.

10. I feel uncomfortable having to work closely with people I find it hard to get along with.

11. I have difficulty dealing with my supervisory responsibilities.

12. I feel under a lot of pressure at work.

13. My stomach ties in knots at work.

14. I think about finding another job.

15. My body becomes tense while I'm working.

16. I believe there is not enough time to get everything done.

17. I feel my work is causing me head pain.

18. It's upsetting having to deal with unrealistic demands made by my supervisor or boss.

19. I don't like having to do things I know are wrong.

20. I don't believe my work is appreciated by my superiors.

Total the number of points. A score of 31 to 49 can be considered the midrange. Toward the upper limits of that range, you may begin to experience more tension than you can cope with constructively. The upper limit, 50 to 60 points, would be considered a high stress level; below 30, a low level of tension.

Stress can grow out of areas of your life other than work. Even happy events can be stressful. Weddings are almost as stressful as divorces. Each of us can tolerate different amounts of stress, but all of us know when the level of stress has risen too high for comfort. Occasionally we can make changes in our lives that cut off the stress at the source. More often, we simply must cope with it.

Stress Breakers

Physical control of stress is very much a matter of learning how to relax. Try any of the following exercises as stress breakers. I've used them with clients so taut they were ready to snap. These exercises calm you down so that you can start up again with energy.

1. Drop your jaw and let your tongue hang limply over your lower teeth. Through your mouth, breathe noisily: "In, 2, 3, 4; Out, 2, 3, 4; In, 2, 3, 4; Out, 2, 3, 4," as if you were beginning to feel the effects of an anesthetic. Your breathing should sound as it would a split second before you began to snore. Be sure you do not pause between the outgoing and incoming breaths. The flow should be constant. Don't stop until you feel a yawn coming on. Yawn and start again.

2. Let your head dangle forward and hang there, eyes closed for six slow counts. Again, counting slowly to six, raise your head from its drooping position until your eyes, gradually opening, see the ceiling. You should feel the tension begin to melt away. Repeat several times.

3. With your head dangling again, let your jaw hang loose, as if it were about to fall out. Roll your head slowly to one side, then back and up, then to the other side, then forward again. (For more Stress Breakers, see some of the anti-nasality exercises in the Appendix.)

8

Social Security

The Art of Conversation
From Self-consciousness to Self-confidence

A lot of business is done at parties and dinners, meetings that on the surface seem purely social. Knowing how to take advantage of the potential in these situations adds to your nine-to-five abilities. Many people aren't at ease in such meetings.

You don't have to be a nobody to worry about having nothing to say when you're meeting somebody. "I find it hard to be in a room full of strangers and hardest of all if many of the strangers know each other," says former First Lady of New York City, Mary Lindsay. "You have to make an effort or it isn't going to work." Mrs. Lindsay says her years as a politician's wife taught her to stick out her hand and introduce herself. "I smile, and if there's no response, I move on to the next person," she says. "If I keep on getting no response, I go home soon."

Tish Baldrige, White House social secretary to Jacqueline Kennedy, and emerging again as a prominent figure in the Reagan social scene in Washington, also has had her moments of panic. "I had to memorize every name in Washington, including all the ambassadors," says Miss Baldrige. "I was constantly stumbling over names when I introduced people, but I learned to live by something Bernard Baruch once said: 'Those who mind don't matter, and those who matter don't mind.'"

Fumbling introductions is a common problem, as is getting things started. It's helpful if you can start people off with a "Sue, this is Jerry. I think, between the two of you, you must spend twenty-four hours a day on the tennis court." As hoary as that old piece of advice is, it works better than leaving two people together with only their names. One ambassador's wife always makes a list of her guests for herself, with a phrase next to each name: "skis at Aspen," "cultivates orchids," "on the opera committee." It's especially useful in getting shy people started. Spending a few minutes longer forging the conversational link between two people you've just introduced—sticking around long enough to make sure they can continue on their own—makes the way even smoother.

What if you have to introduce two people and—horror of horrors—your mind draws a blank on one of their names? Laugh at yourself, make a joking reference to your lapse, and everyone will relax. "Since I don't know my own name nowadays, how can I remember hers?" The person whose name you're trying desperately to recall probably will come to your rescue.

Mrs. Lindsay and Miss Baldrige have their own solutions for making themselves at ease in social situations. For most people the key to social ease is to follow a few simple hints for conversation. Back in Chapter 2, when I mentioned the five message givers, I left out one very important one. How you say what you say is very important, but no less so is what you say. How you choose to express your ideas is a reflection of the quality of your thinking, and nothing contributes more to presence than the ability to talk about worthwhile things and events in a worthwhile way.

THE ART OF CONVERSATION

Good conversation can be exhilarating, help you get ahead, solve your problems, increase your knowledge. Good conversation can even help you lose weight. Once at dinner I sat next to a prominent lawyer who I knew had had a heart attack not long before. The dinner was a buffet, and the lawyer piled his plate high. I thought to myself, "He shouldn't eat all that. Maybe he won't eat as much if I get him talking about something he's interested in." So I asked him about the merits of two political rivals, and he became so involved in conversation that the rest of us had about finished by the time he lifted his fork. He only had time to nibble.

There are a few simple secrets to the art of conversation. If you use them, you'll enjoy being with others more, because they'll enjoy you more.

Conversational Style

Bill Moyers and David Frost are paid to make conversation, and they're excellent examples for those who want to be better conversationalists. Moyers and Frost probe without prying, they search deeply without offending, they show interest, concern, empathy, and understanding as they try to gain insight into and information from their subjects.

But you needn't be a professional interviewer to be a good conversationalist. All of us know people whose presence lights up a room, who have a green thumb with people. At a conference table, they start a flow of ideas; at a dinner party, they stimulate and make *you* sparkle with more than your usual luster. A good conversationalist tries in a thousand subtle ways to get to know you—what you like, what you hate, what makes you the person you are.

Truman Capote is said to turn down thirty-five dinner invitations a week. "Truman gets along with everyone," says one of his friends, "because he finds everybody fascinating, from society types to cops. When he talks to you, it's a very personal experience. You can feel him taking it all in." Mr. Capote's explanation is simpler. "I refuse to be bored," he says.

"People," said André Malraux, "often can be measured by the questions they ask." Good conversation involves offering your listener an opening; frequently that's a question that requires the sort of answer that carries a conversation forward. If you ask, "How was your trip?" you may get "Fine" for an answer. If you ask, "What did you find most rewarding about your two weeks in South Africa?" you will have brought the other person into a conversation with you. "Why would you like to see John as chairman of the board?" is likely to net you considerably more information and interest than "Do you think John will be chairman?"

Draw others out with questions like:

Why would a . . .
What do you think will . . .
In your opinion what .
How did you happen to .   .
Could you give me a for instance?

Food for Thought

Have interesting things to say. You can if you keep replenishing
your thought larder as you do your refrigerator. If you have nothing to say, maybe that's because you haven't looked at the world
lately. If you don't have time to read a daily newspaper thoroughly, read the editorials—they always provide topics for talk.
Go through at least one of the news magazines each week—that
way you'll have something to contribute on almost any topic of
conversation that comes up. Read a special interest magazine for
depth—one in an area that interests you and could interest others.
And try to at least scan another magazine that covers the arts, theater, entertainment.

When you're getting ready for an occasion at which you'll be
talking something other than business, get your mind ready too.
Keep a TV or radio news program on while you're dressing, and
collect tidbits that will make for interesting exchanges—an event,
crisis, public concern.

Edit Your Conversation

Knowing what not to talk about is as important as knowing what
to talk about. For starters, leave out children, illness, personal
gripes, sports exploits, recipes. I can remember one Christmas day
at a friend's house when the after-dinner conversation couldn't be
wrested away from two people who made the Cuisinart the subject
of an hour's discussion. The nonstop talker, the repeater, the
rambler, the overdetailer all are conversation killers. So is the ego-
rapt rapper, the monopolizer. Bores, said A. A. Milne, can be
divided into two classes: those who have their own particular subject, and those who need no subject.

Some people are so entertaining that everyone *wants* them to
keep on talking. But even the most gifted raconteur should keep an
eye out for boredom, irritation, and frustration. If your listeners
truly are enchanted, they'll keep flashing the "go" signal. Don't stay

on stage too long. As George Jessel said, if you don't strike oil in the first three minutes, stop boring.

Conversation Killers

Women may lean toward overtalking, but men are more guilty of killing conversation, reports sociologist Pamela Fishman. She also has found that women put more effort into keeping a conversation going—even though they have less control over what the conversation is about. In 150 hours of male-female conversations she recorded and analyzed, reports Fishman, topics introduced by the men succeeded in becoming developed further 96 percent of the time. Women initiated 62 percent of the topics but succeeded in getting them talked about only 36 percent of the time.

According to Fishman, the women used a number of positive strategies. Women asked questions nearly three times as often as men did. One way men killed conversational topics was by giving minimal responses like "um," a grunt, "good." Blunt one-word aborters are death to conversation.

Sociologists Candace West and Donald Zimmerman of the University of California at Santa Barbara report that men also interrupt more than women do. The two researchers recorded and analyzed conversations in a variety of university settings—a coffee shop, a drugstore, an apartment. They found that men interrupted women much more often than they interrupted other men, and much more often than women interrupted either sex. The patterns, West and Zimmerman said, were similar to those they'd observed in an earlier study of parents and children—the parents behaving like the men in the college study.

Interrupting is a conversation killer. Only when a speaker is putting people to sleep, when he is antagonizing or being seriously offensive, when, in short, he's become a social nuisance, is the interruption a conversation rescuer.

Tact

Tact is diplomacy of the heart. It means saying the right thing at the right time, and also leaving unsaid the wrong thing at the tempting moment. Disraeli explained his popularity with Queen Victoria: "I never deny. I never contradict. I sometimes forget." Sensitivity to the feelings of others will tell you whether a subject is risky or safe, depending on the people around you and the mood of the moment. Race, religion, or politics may be rewarding in some groups and lethal in others.

Tact is editing. When to and when not to. What to and what not to. It means not invading others' privacy, avoiding the personal, prying, petty question, shunning gossip. Ninety percent of conversation is chitchat, revolving around people and personalities. Most of us would find conversation totally without personalities as dull as an egg without salt. Our greatest interest outside ourselves is other people. And why not? But to pass on hurtful facts or allegations maliciously, or in order to boost your ego by appearing privy to things others don't know, reflects back on you negatively. " 'Tis best to leave the sins of others well alone," wrote Montaigne, "until you've made some headway of your own."

Discussion is fruitful; argument is hurtful. "Good talk in people's homes fell off terribly for several years," complained Norman Podhoretz, editor of *Commentary*. "The reason, of course, was that we all had become so highly politicized—to one extreme or another. Up until recently, if you wanted to run a salon, you had to worry about who could be put in the same room with whom. People with opposite viewpoints couldn't stand each other and conversation came to an absolute standstill."

So long as tempers remain cool and reason and good humor reign, so long as you are willing to listen to me and I am willing to hear you out, so long as we direct ourselves to the issues rather than to passion or prejudice, then discussion has not degenerated into quarreling.

Listening

At a Washington party recently, I was standing and talking with a politician who shall remain nameless. I was facing him—and the room. He was facing me and the wall. After a while he said, "You know, I can't help remarking how amazing it is that instead of looking the room over while we're talking, your eyes haven't once stopped listening to me. And I know there must be a dozen bigger social lions behind me."

Half of good conversation is listening—not with just your ears, but with your eyes too. If you don't look at the speaker, you don't know what his eyes are saying. And they can say a lot.

It's easy, when the talk is less than dynamic, to find yourself thinking of something else, to miss key words and phrases, to misinterpret what you hear, to decide in advance what point is being made and fail to notice when it turns out to be a different point altogether. Listening attentively gives you grace. The greatest compliment you can pay anyone is really to listen to what he has to say.

And answer responsively, unlike Gary Cooper, a gentleman known for his taciturnity, who once was interviewed about an upcoming film. "Is it true, Mr. Cooper, that Grace Kelly will be your co-star?"

"Yup," replied Cooper, without embellishment.

"And the plot revolves around certain moral issues?" continued the reporter.

"Yup."

Several other questions followed, and all were met with the same terse answer. Finally the reporter exasperatedly asked, "Mr. Cooper, is 'Yup' the only word you know?"

"Nope," answered Cooper.

The rhythm of good conversation is like the rhythm of a good tennis volley—send and receive, send and receive. Listening is half of good conversation, but talking is still the other half.

FROM SELF-CONSCIOUSNESS TO SELF-CONFIDENCE

When Billy Rose first came to New York, he lived in a rented room in an old brownstone in the West Forties. His window looked out on a dark courtyard. One day, when he was having his breakfast at the corner drugstore, a young man walked over to him and said, "I can never thank you enough." Rose was startled. "What for?" he asked. "I've never seen you before in my life."

"I have the room across the courtyard from yours," the man said, "and I was very sick with pneumonia and I didn't think I'd make it. From my bed I could see your windowsill with the geranium on it and I said to myself, 'If that geranium can survive in this dark hole, so can I.'"

Billy, in telling me that story years later, said, "I didn't have the heart to tell him it was an artificial geranium."

Sometimes things are not what they are, but what they seem. Changing your attitude about yourself can liberate you from shackles of shyness and feelings of inadequacy. Changing your attitude about yourself is the key to projecting authority and confidence.

I always was painfully shy. In college, I'd raise my hand to answer a question, and then freeze when the professor called on me. I could not get the answer out. In the theater, I was totally self-confident on stage, but that was because I was playing someone else. Off stage, as Dorothy Sarnoff, I suffered agonizing self-consciousness. Then one day I was a guest of honor, along with Steve Allen and Eleanor Roosevelt, at a United Nations Day ceremony. I had met Mrs. Roosevelt several times before, and I'd always admired her ease with people. I told her so.

"I wasn't always that much at ease," she replied. She used to be self-conscious about being so tall, and she had thought she was ugly. "A friend told me I had the wrong attitude about myself. She said, 'You're seeing yourself as tall, awkward, ugly. That's wrong. You are tall and important, the queen of this country. Why don't you act as though you are wearing a crown?' That's what I tried to do —and the deception worked."

I tried out a version of Mrs. Roosevelt's device at a birthday party Yul Brynner and I gave for Gertrude Lawrence—we all were in *The King and I* at the time. That was the beginning of my Attitude Adjustment formula, which hasn't failed me since. Yul and I invited Gertrude's friends—Marlene Dietrich, Noel Coward, and dozens of other stars. I told myself that in that company I couldn't wear a queen's crown. But if I wasn't a great star, I had been quite successful in the theater. I would try to think of myself as wearing a smaller crown.

If that sounds like deception, it was deception that worked. I walked into the party, for the first time self-confident at a gathering. The words of a song from the show ran through my mind: "Whenever I feel afraid, I hold my head erect, and whistle a happy tune, so no one will suspect I'm afraid."

I've taught many people to wear their own special crowns. You can wear one too.

According to one study, about 40 percent of us, or eighty-five million Americans, consider ourselves shy. Among those who admit they whistle happy tunes are Barbara Walters, Henry Fonda, Gloria Steinem, James Mason, and Oscar de la Renta. Marvin Belli, the outrageous attorney, says he "became flamboyant to hide shyness." Ann-Margret says it's not easy to hide her shyness when "I'm being me." Even Don Rickles admits to feeling unsure about himself: "You can have a fear of rejection when you're out there and all you have to sell is yourself." Carol Burnett, Prince Charles, and Catherine Deneuve are among others in the limelight who say they once were painfully shy.

Except for those people who, in psychiatric jargon, overcompensate, who turn their personalities on the flip side and become unusually gregarious, the shy person is timid. He speaks sparingly and then in a soft voice. He constantly wonders: What are others thinking? Why do I feel so uncomfortable? He tries desperately to hide his physical signs of nervousness: the pounding heart, racing pulse, quivering voice, trembling, sweating, blushing.

Shyness, or self-consciousness, is a syndrome—fear that others will disapprove of or laugh at you, feelings of unworthiness, embarrassment, self-rejection. The symptoms are not unlike what basically un-shy people experience when they have to give a talk. The difference is that shy or self-conscious people have symptoms of uneasiness even when the talk is just a chat with another person.

Almost the same method of Attitude Adjusting that works to conquer nervousness and put you at ease in a public appearance can help you conquer social self-consciousness.

The first step is to take a more objective and realistic look at yourself and to force yourself to acknowledge your positive qualities, exactly as you did in the exercise in Chapter 1. Go back to that list now and come up with thirty positive qualities; give yourself the benefit of any doubts.

The second step is to follow the guidelines to good conversation. That will prepare you to function well in almost any arena.

The third step is to begin to think positively about your goals of self-improvement. Stop criticizing yourself. Declare:

"I'm going to have interesting things to talk about."
"I'm going to introduce myself to others at the party."
"I'm going to contribute an idea or two at the next meeting."
"I'm going to lose ten pounds."

You can change overnight. If you follow the suggestions I've used with success on over sixty thousand people, you will give yourself confidence, authority, presence, and power. The formula should be clear by now:

> Anticipate.
> Prepare.
> Put into practice.
> Most important of all—Attitude Adjust!

Viktor Frankl, a man who survived the Nazi concentration camps, said he was able to endure his imprisonment because he realized that "the last of human freedoms is the ability to choose one's attitude."

You have the freedom to choose your attitude. Exercise it!

9

You're on Television

I met Mrs. Begin before I met the Prime Minister. I had been asked to go to Jerusalem to consult with Mr. Begin and see what I could do to change the Prime Minister's style of responding to television interviewers. The Camp David summit was approaching, and fresh in everyone's mind was Mr. Begin's less than affable performance on "Face the Nation."

In the foyer of the Begins' modest house, I was met by a short woman puffing on a cigarette. "What are you going to do with my husband?" Mrs. Begin asked in a husky Lauren Bacall voice.

"What would you like me to do with him?" I answered warmly.

"My husband doesn't need anything," Mrs. Begin said. "We made it through all of those terrible times all the way to Prime Minister, and we did it with deeds, not cosmetic maneuvers."

Before I left New York, I had suggested that Mr. Begin get rid of the heavy black-rimmed glasses that made him look almost sinister. That had been taken care of by the time I got to Israel; he now was wearing a much lighter frame. I also had commented that the Prime Minister's shirts were too large in the neck. A too-large shirt makes a man look as though he's lost a lot of weight recently, which can translate as, "He must be very ill." I had called Israel before I left New York and had got the Prime Minister's proper neck size and sleeve length. My husband, Milton, had picked out several shirts and ties at Saks and Sulka. We had carried them to Israel in our luggage.

"It's different on American television," I said to Mrs. Begin after a while. "Here your husband is a hero." I selected two simple blue shirts and ties to match and gave them to Mrs. Begin, trying to make them a belated birthday present to her husband. "This is for the Prime Minister's birthday," I said.

"My husband always wears white shirts," Mrs. Begin smiled. "He never wears anything but white shirts."

I tried. "Mrs. Begin, blue shirts are so much better on television than white . . ." I could not bring myself to mention Anwar el-Sadat, who clearly had mastered dressing for the medium, as her husband had not.

"But he always wears white shirts!" Mrs. Begin insisted.

"He also should have a blue suit."

"Blue suit? But he's got two suits."

"I've made an appointment with your best Jerusalem tailor," I said.

"Why a tailor?" Mrs. Begin asked. "We buy his suits off the rack."

We visited the tailor. My husband by now had almost managed to charm the Prime Minister's wife. "Mrs. Begin," he said, "feel this fabric. Isn't it wonderful?" She agreed.

"He's going to Camp David," said my husband. "He really ought to have a pair of slacks."

"Slacks!" objected Mrs. Begin. "My husband doesn't wear slacks."

My own husband switched tactics. "How about a gray flannel suit? Then in case the Prime Minister wants to, he can take off the jacket and a sweater will look fine on top of them."

"How can the tailor make a suit for my husband?" she asked. "He has no time for fittings."

"Give me one of the Prime Minister's suits," my husband suggested. "I'll bring it back here. The tailor will take the measurements of the suit. He can copy the style from a simple suit of my own."

Outside the building that housed the Prime Minister's offices, a guard with a gun searched my purse. In the lobby, another guard with a gun did the same, as other visitors checked their own weapons at the desk. But the first thing that struck me about the Prime Minister's offices themselves was the extraordinary calm, an unexpected haven of peace. It reflected the serious serenity of people proceeding in so intelligent and organized a fashion that there is no need for hurry or noise.

And everyone was smiling. Everyone acted as if he had all the time in the world for me; as I walked down the corridor, every office door was open.

I met first with several of Mr. Begin's staff, among them Yehuda, his chief speechwriter, and Yona, the Prime Minister's press secretary who had been with Mr. Begin for five years, a protective, loyal, and warm woman.

I asked the group a battery of questions: Who has personal influence with him? Who has the strongest political influence? Can he laugh at himself? What is his tolerance for listening to other people? What is his tolerance for correction? What kind of cooperation can I expect from him? What are his strongest convictions and passions?

I asked what they had thought of the Prime Minister's appearance on "Face the Nation." "It did not do him justice."

The Prime Minister had had an excessively troubled day. And just as the program had been about to start, the moderator had instructed him: "Now, Mr. Prime Minister, you sit here and you look into the camera so, and you . . ." The Prime Minister, his aides said, was bothered by being treated as though he never had appeared on a television show before. He also was upset by a question one reporter asked about his health.

"Is there anything about handling interviews you think he wants in particular to know about?" I asked.

"He really doesn't know where to look when he's on a television show," one of Mr. Begin's aides answered.

I laid down my conditions. "He's not going to work well with a guard in the room who'll hear me correct him," I said. "I'd like to work alone with him."

"Of course," they said.

Condition number two, I said, was that I did not want to be brought in to meet him. He would come to my room, with me standing in front of my camera, and meet me.

Just as the Prime Minister was about to enter, Mrs. Begin

telephoned. "I really owe you an apology," she said. "That was no way to greet you this morning. Would you please come by and have a cup of coffee when you are finished with my husband?"

The Prime Minister walked in, and I extended my arms. "At last," I said.

"So what are you going to do with me?" he asked.

"What do you want me to do?"

He didn't answer.

"I hear you're not sure where to look when you're doing an interview," I said. "Is that true?"

"Yes," he said.

"Isn't it simply common sense?" I asked. "You speak directly into the eyes of the interviewer."

"How's the camera going to—" he began.

"It's the camera's job to follow you and pick up your eyes," I answered. "But I'm going to tell your staff that there's a better camera angle for you. They must protect you and see that the camera angle is lower so that we can see your eyes. With the camera above you, the rims of your glasses hide your eyes when it's most important for us to feel your sincerity, conviction, and strength."

"Ah," said the Prime Minister. "Interesting."

I mentioned that blue shirts photographed better on television and that I had left two of them at his home as a birthday present for him.

"I always wear white shirts," he said. "But I'll ask my wife. If she says I can wear blue shirts, I'll wear blue shirts."

We began our session by videotaping an interview. I started with relatively simple questions: "In your book, you say you don't use power, you use only moral influence. But, Mr. Prime Minister, isn't that just another term for power?" "What you did in the past was a piece of cake compared to what can only be frustration and stalemate in the future. Can Israel really ever be free of the fear of being annihilated? Ever?" "Mr. Prime Minister, isn't it true that Israel is sitting in the middle of an arena with no escape exits? Look at your own map up here on the wall. Show me your escape route if the Arab nations all band together against you."

Then I asked the question that had so thrown him on his "Face the Nation" interview: "Mr. Prime Minister, it is rumored that you are in very bad health, and indeed there is some question about your mental health." He laughed nervously, just as he had on the program, and struggled again through an unconvincing answer.

"If you answer it that way," I said, "they'll go for the jugular. What do you have against showing your strength and saying, 'Like millions of people all over the world, and like two of your own Presidents, I had a coronary, and I'm fully recovered. I feel fine, and my doctor says that I'm in excellent health.'"

"Can I mention the word 'coronary' on the air?" he asked.

"Look what it does for you," I answered him. "You control the situation. You protect yourself by that answer."

"I never thought of it that way," he said. With that, we ended our session.

I returned to the Prime Minister's home. Mrs. Begin was sitting in the breakfast room playing with the envelope that held the fabric swatches. "We're very simple people," she said again. "My husband has two suits. And anyway, he has no time for fittings."

The next morning, I called Mr. Heidlich, the tailor, and asked him if he was ready for a fitting. He said emphatically that he was not. I told him I had to sneak him in that day. I said, "Bring as much as you've got stitched together."

They ushered Mr. Heidlich into the office fifteen minutes before Mr. Begin and I were scheduled to start. The jacket he brought had no sleeves, but the rest was basted together. "Mr. Heidlich, come," I said, and I sat him down next to the television monitor so that he almost melted into it. "Mr. Heidlich," I said, "now don't be upset by anything that happens. Don't be upset by the way he talks to you. He has a lot on his mind."

"Don't worry," said Mr. Heidlich. "My grandfather was Archduke Ferdinand's tailor. I know how to handle this."

Mr. Begin came in beaming. I beamed back and said, "We're going to begin by taking off your jacket." I threw out a quick introduction. The Prime Minister stood there growing apoplectic, but I was talking so furiously, he could not get a word in. "Mr. Heidlich," I chattered, "the button is too high. Mr. Prime Minister, you know how television is . . ." It can't have taken more than three minutes.

The Prime Minister was wearing a blue shirt, not one that I had brought. "My wife says I can wear blue shirts," he said, "but not a striped tie."

We began our session. I had asked one of the Prime Minister's aides to play interviewer and to pitch difficult questions to Mr. Begin. "Oh, no," Yehuda said. "You're going back to America, but I have to stay here. He'll never forgive me." I persuaded three other members of the staff to take the adversary role.

We did an entire twenty-seven-minute television show. The questions were brilliant, the Prime Minister's performance considerably improved. But I kept sending notes to the interviewers: "Press him, press him to the wall. Don't be satisfied. Press." Finally we asked the Prime Minister the question about his health. Again we got the embarrassed laugh and the verbal detour.

I switched off the camera. "Okay," I said to the Prime Minister. "You get one more try on the question of your health."

He didn't quite make it the second time either, but the third time around he gave a straight answer. "I feel so much better about it," he said afterward. "I'm in control and I got rid of it."

"This is a terrific game," the Prime Minister said when we had finished. "We were so stupid. We just sat around thinking of questions that could be asked. But you don't get the same feeling of pressure; it's an entirely different kind of timing. Isn't it wonderful to know you still can be taught."

Then he asked me, "Tell me, what do you think of Sadat on television?"

"Well, Mr. Prime Minister," I non-answered, "do you realize that he's gone through the same kind of thing you just did?"

"Really?" said Mr. Begin. He honestly had not known.

There was one other thing I had planned to do with the Prime Minister. I had with me a tape of his "Face the Nation" interview. But now I re-evaluated. I had Mr. Begin thinking positively about how he would handle his next interview on American television. Reviewing his dreadful past performance might be demoralizing. And he was about to leave for Camp David. So despite all the trouble we had taken to get the tape, I decided to skip it.

After our session, the Prime Minister met with my husband and two of our friends. The three American men wore blue shirts—our conspiracy. But in the end, all the blue shirts and expensive ties we had brought wound up going to Mr. Begin's aides. The Prime Minister had the best-dressed staff at Camp David, but I never again saw Mr. Begin himself in a blue shirt.

The next day I met once more with the Prime Minister's staff. "You have to protect him in many ways," I said. "You have to go to the studio ahead of time and arrange that he has full front lighting. Side lighting makes him look sinister. See that his tie is straight. Keep reminding him to charm, charm."

I wrote copious memos, then spent hours editing them. I had to make the material brief enough so they would not say, "This is too long," and toss it aside.

Finally I boiled everything down to three pages. I pondered the best way to give the Prime Minister what he needed without pointing a finger at him. In the end I wrote on the page: "You may be interested in some of the guidelines for leaders of foreign nations who must appear on American television that will be included in my next book."

The last sentence on my memorandum to the Prime Minister was: "If you must use the iron fist, put on a velvet glove." That was the line, one of his staff told me later, that the Prime Minister remembered the best. When, nearly a year later, Barbara Walters was inordinately adversary with Mr. Begin during a television interview, he smiled at her benevolently. "Now, Barbara," he said softly, "you don't really want to use that tone of voice with me, do you?"

IT CAN HAPPEN TO YOU

Until recently, most people who weren't politicians or actors assumed it never would happen to them, unless perhaps they got caught by "Candid Camera." But with the constant increase in the number of local talk shows, the growth of Cable TV and satellite transmission, and the trend toward using video in business (and even in the courtroom in place of live witnesses), it's likely that a television appearance is in your future.

Doctors, lawyers, teachers, business people, and authors are appearing on television these days. Nothing sells like the exposure to millions that TV offers, but most people do not know how to present themselves to their advantage. Few people are naturals on the airwaves—even the professionals.

Paul, an investment adviser, had written an excellent book on beating the stock market and was sent to me by his skeptical publisher to be groomed for television. Paul was petrified by the thought of it all. When he played out a mock television interview, he sat curled up fetus-like, scarcely able to mumble a word.

For starters I asked him to rearrange himself in the chair and sit upright, inclined slightly forward. Then I showed him how to control nervousness through the vital triangle contractions. Then I indoctrinated him with the "I'm glad I'm here . . ." chant.

In the role of interviewer, I began again with easy questions, then went on to tougher ones. Next I asked him the questions he said he hoped they wouldn't ask him: "How much of the time have you been right?" "If you're so good, how many millions have you made?"

We worked on those squirmers until no question bothered him. His book and his TV tour were a huge success, and he's just written a new bestseller and is currently taking a refresher course. But he knows now that a television guest's objective is to promote something, and that a television show's objective is to engage or entertain.

Anticipation

The usual reaction to an invitation to appear on television is delight at having been asked followed immediately by terror. A biologist client said he pictured himself under a magnifying glass that would broadcast his defects to the world; like almost everybody else, he was concentrating on his inadequacies. If you weren't knowledgeable, you wouldn't have been invited. Television producers are besieged by agents desperate to get their clients on; you were chosen because you have something special to contribute.

Prepare intelligently by doing your homework. If you're not familiar with the program, find out when, where, and to what kind of audience it's broadcast. Find out how long you'll be on, who will interview you, whether you'll be on with other guests and who they are. Will a makeup person and/or a hairdresser be available (both male and female guests use those services)? Will the segment be broadcast live, or taped and edited? Henry Kissinger once canceled an appearance at the last minute because he couldn't get the right to approve an edited interview.

Try to watch the show in advance. Does the director take mostly tight close-up shots? Evaluate the interviewer—there are distinct differences. Dr. Gerald Klein, a U.C.L.A. psychologist and communications expert, dissected the TV interview styles of Carson, Cavett, Donahue, Douglas, Griffin, Shore, and Snyder. Phil Donahue, who uses the broadest range of responses to a guest, came away with the highest marks from Dr. Klein. He dubbed Merv Griffin "the innocuous question king." Dr. Klein says there are only a few basic responses by a host to a guest's statement:

• A question, to get more information.
• A request for more information.
• Silence—which lets messages sink in and avoids verbal crowding.
• Reflection—paraphrasing the guest's message to show empathy or understanding.
• Self-disclosure—revealing the interviewer's own thoughts, behavior, or feelings, which heightens intimacy.

You may not draw a superb interviewer like Phil Donahue or Barbara Walters or Bill Moyers. Some interviewers are well-informed and well-prepared; others wing it on charm. Some are abrasive and challenging. Others are unthreateningly curious and fair. A lazy or unintelligent interviewer is more difficult than a well-prepared and intelligent one. Be prepared for all kinds.

Few television guests realize they can protect themselves by making reasonable requests. When I was invited on "The Tomorrow Show," I watched the program before my appearance. Tom Snyder, the host, at six feet four inches, looked fine in one of the set's padded red-leather oversized lounge chairs. I knew they would overwhelm me. I also saw that the lighting on the guests' faces was unflattering side lighting, and that the director favored tight close-ups. I asked to have the lighting full-front on my face, a straight chair, and no shots tighter than head-to-waist. The producer was kind enough to oblige.

I observed that Snyder prepared about four questions for each guest—enough for the articulate but not for the timid. I knew I'd need to be ready with lots to say if I wanted to make the interview pay off. My objective was to interest executive viewers and inform them that my speechmaking techniques were available on a series of cassette tapes.

When I arrived at the studio, I found Tom Snyder sitting in a straight-backed chair; it was as good for him as it was for me. I reminded the director about avoiding close-ups. "Indulge me," I smiled. "I'll be so much more comfortable with waist shots." The lighting was what I had requested.

The show could not have gone better. Within the next few weeks we received more than a thousand orders for the cassettes, and today people still are calling up and mentioning that show when they inquire about our services.

Preparation

Once you know you're going to be on TV, prepare to practice, or role-play. For one of his first speeches after he took office, Gerald Ford taped and retaped the twenty-five-minute broadcast over a period of four days. Even so, when he finally went on, his Teleprompter carried not only the text but also directorial instructions such as "stand up," "sit down," and "change camera." President Reagan was equally indefatigable at role-playing for his debate with President Carter.

The most important thing to keep in mind as you practice is whatever it is that you don't want to go off the air without having said. You may not be asked a leading question; you have to be prepared to create your own opportunity to get that information in.

Find a friend who will role-play the interviewer with you and tape-record your sessions. Your friend should start with easy and obvious questions, then move on to more difficult ones. Switch roles and play the interviewer yourself; you may come up with some stumpers you'd overlooked. This kind of anticipation will keep you cool in the hot seat later.

Think of the worst possible questions, and have your mock interviewer ask them until you're confident you've found the best possible answers. Most of the time you know what the question is before it's finished; practice formulating your answers as soon as you know. Don't wait until your interviewer has finished speaking to start thinking.

Shape your answer by forming your conclusion first; work back from that to establish linking sentences that take you from the question to your main message, like a basketball player who keeps his eye on the basket while dribbling the ball toward it.

Suppose the interviewer asks: "Miss Robinette, your book seems to blame men for everything that's wrong with society. Do you really think that's fair?" Your target is to end with a statement strongly critical of our materialistic society. You proceed: "My book deals with an issue larger than gender. It's an examination of all the factors that create the problems we find increasingly difficult to solve. The basic one, in my opinion, is the emphasis on consumerism at the expense of conservation." Never repeat a negative comment in your answer; that only reinforces it to your viewers. Miss Robinette would be making a mistake if she repeated the phrase "blame men for everything."

Speak conversationally, animatedly, as though you were in a spirited discussion at home or at work. Watch interviews on television—especially those broadcast Sundays, when the most intelligent fare seems to be served up. Analyze the qualities of the best guests and the worst.

HOW TO LOOK GOOD ON CAMERA

A famous golfer with several million dollars' worth of advertising endorsement contracts was about to lose his sponsors because he looked so wooden and indifferent in his commercials. Instead of seeming enthusiastic and exuding "belief in product," he looked monumentally bored. In private he was cheerful and charming; in public he was painfully shy. (I even had to show him how to relate to the galleries, which he ignored at the championship matches because they broke his concentration.) Hardly the personality you'd want endorsing your product. We animated his face and gave him the "I'm glad I'm here, I'm glad you're here" phrases. In two hours his face had come alive and so had his commercial. If your face lacks animation, repeating those phrases will put light behind your face as the camera introduces you to the home viewers.

Sitting erect makes you look younger, slimmer, and generally more attractive; slouching makes you look apathetic and withdrawn. Cross your legs, one knee over the other. If you have short thighs or heavy ones, or if you're a woman and when you read this the mini is back in fashion, sit with your legs pressed tightly together from thighs to ankles, both feet on the floor and angled three or four inches to the side. (Pressing your legs together, uncrossed, makes them look slimmer.)

Your hands look best clasped loosely in your lap, slightly behind your kneecaps. If you have trouble keeping your hands still, dig the thumbnail of one hand into the palm of the other. Besides reminding you to keep your hands still, that acts as an isometric exercise and helps you maintain your body intensity.

The last step in your preparation is deciding what to wear. Avoid black or white. If you've seen the set, avoid also any color that clashes with it or that matches it too closely. Before one televised speech, a gold drape was hung behind Richard Nixon's desk in the Oval Office. Evidently the staff thought the golden backdrop would add a desirable touch of pomp. Unfortunately, on home screens, the gold turned to beige, and Nixon's badly made-up face melted right into it.

A dark blue suit conveys the most authority; a light blue or pale colored shirt or a shirt with a subtle stripe and a small-patterned or subtly striped tie look best. As I've noted before, the fit of your collar and the width of your shirt cuffs are important; a collar pin can make you look stuffy. Avoid glasses that reflect light (specially treated nonglare glasses are available); do without glasses altogether if you can without squinting.

Most women do well in vibrant colors—I favor French blue and red for myself. Nancy Reagan and Lesley Stahl apparently feel the same way I do about red. Avoid a bare throat, shiny metal jewelry that "burns" the camera lens, dangling earrings, and clanking jewelry—microphones can magnify the sound into the crash of coal rushing down a tin chute.

When you've decided what you're going to wear, take a look at yourself in a mirror—sitting. See that your skirt doesn't ride up too high; slit skirts and cleavage are distracting; a dress gathered at the waist can make you look enormous. Some jackets bunch up on the shoulders when you move; for both women and men, the jacket should fit smoothly on the shoulders. A buttoned jacket gives a man a look of greater authority. Socks should be dark and long enough to cover the entire lower leg; I'll never forget the distraction of Peter Drucker's bare legs when his white socks slipped down around his ankles as he sat with crossed legs.

If you can arrange to have a run-through with a television consultant, that may make you more comfortable. In our office TV studio, we videotape a mock interview, see what there is to improve, and then do another run-through. Whether or not you're able to do that, you can do what our clients do before they go on —prepare a few 6 × 9 index cards with notes printed in black felt-tip pen reminding them of the messages they want to deliver on the air and a few anecdotes they can use to make their points.

AT THE TELEVISION STUDIO

When you arrive (on time) you'll probably go right to the makeup room, where shiny bald heads are matted down, jowls and noses darkened and minimized. If there's no hairdresser, check your hair yourself, and ask the makeup person for hairspray, if necessary. One chief of a government agency was upstaged during an entire program by a bouncing cowlick; no one could concentrate on his message.

The studio itself usually is as high and wide as an airplane hangar, and frequently it's a scene of controlled chaos. Technicians scurry around, lights are adjusted, cameras roll like dinosaurs across the set, trailing fat rubber cables. The floor often is a web of wires, tape, and chalk marks. People wearing earphones hustle about with clipboards.

The pace is frantic; nobody pays much attention to you; you may feel like a product on a conveyor belt. Keep calm in all this frenzy by Attitude Adjusting—tightening your vital triangle and repeating your "I'm glad I'm here" litany until the countdown comes. You may derive some extra calm from noticing that your interviewer looks about as nervous as you feel.

The microphone will be hung around your neck or clipped onto your dress or jacket. If it's attached to your tie, ask the technician to make sure your tie is straight and the knot up to the collar; a tie askew is very distracting. And if you're seated in a swivel chair, ask to have it locked so that you don't swivel unthinkingly.

You'll feel the lights very hot. The floor director signals: "Ten seconds!"

Facing Your Unseen Audience

Television interviews last from six to twenty minutes. In general, give short answers—three or four sentences. That cuts down on the chance that your words will be edited out of context if it's a taped show.

Keep your face animated and the love apples in your cheeks

even when you're listening. Look into the eyes of the person with whom you're speaking; it's the camera's job to find you and your eyes, not vice versa. If you want at some point to give the folks at home a message, though, say so, and look directly at the camera; imagine that the lens has two eyes and that they're the eyes of your mother who's hanging on your every word.

Speak in your lowest possible pitch—it's more attractive over a microphone. Britain's Prime Minister Margaret Thatcher learned to speak several notes lower to be at her best on the medium. Speak with energy and momentum. If your interviewer is apathetic, don't emulate his pacing or tone. Be conscious of the rhythm of interchange—keep your replies brief. Edit yourself, and if you're one of a group, don't monopolize.

If you don't know the answer to a question, say so, don't hedge. Don't use your interviewer's name more than two or three times— overuse projects a false sort of intimacy.

And what if you're asked a prickly question you overlooked during your rehearsals? As David Brinkley commented, "When a reporter asks questions, he isn't working for the person being questioned, whether businessman, politician, or bureaucrat. He's working for the readers or listeners." Answer briefly and slip quickly into a statement you want to make (Q: "Is it true that you haven't sponsored one important bill, Senator?" A: "I've worked hard for many important pieces of legislation. For example . . ."). If you have a devilish adversary, and if you've observed that he buries his nose in his notes when it's your turn to reply, you might try the stratagem George Bush once used on Mike Wallace. In the midst of a grilling, Bush realized that Wallace studied his notes as soon as he'd finished asking a question and the camera was off him. On the next question, Bush replied with a tumbler, a one-word answer—"No." The camera instantly returned to Wallace for the next question and caught him off guard and unprepared.

Watch out for interviewers who like to trip up their guests by waiting for the last seconds and then insisting that a hostile question be answered with a yes or no, "because we're running out of time." If that happens, remember that the television studio isn't a courtroom. If yes or no won't do you justice, say pleasantly but firmly, "I'm sorry that we don't have time for me to give you a proper answer to that question." Don't dissemble unless you have to protect a negotiation. Avoid "I'm glad you asked me that . . ." and other stalls. And again, remember not to repeat a negative in your answer. Don't let the viewer hear words like "company losses," "government deficit," or "incompetence" twice.

If you are intelligently prepared, you will know that you have helped the camera help you make the most of your best.

Last-minute Review

Here is a reminder list my clients use when they're scheduled to be on a television show:

1. Watch the program in advance for interviewer style.

2. Role-play at least two days before the program, first as the interviewer, then as yourself. Use a tape recorder.

3. Note on index cards several points you want to be sure to cover on the air.

4. If the interviewer isn't taking you where you want to go, be assertive. Control your own interview even if that sometimes means you'll be doing a short monologue.

5. You'll do a stronger interview if you tune up your pacing and energizing on a tape recorder before going to the television station.

6. If you don't think tight shots do you justice, request that the camera not close in on you. It's your face.

7. Don't lounge and look overrelaxed. Sitting upright, torso inclined slightly forward, makes you look more enthusiastic, alert, interested.

8. Animate!
Energize!
Light up your face!!!

9. Attitude Adjust. "I'm glad I'm here, I'm glad you're here, I care about you, I know that I know." Do slow exhalations. Keep contracting the vital triangle muscles back toward your spine as you listen and talk.

CORPORATE VIDEO

A title appears on the screen: "State of the Company Address." The deep, resonant voice of a well-known television announcer intones: "This is a presentation of the XYZ Corporation on its worldwide video network." We see a close-up of the vice-president for public relations; he stares out at us as wooden and empty-eyed as an extra from *The Night of the Walking Dead*. The Mummy introduces the president and the chairman. The three men sit around a barrel-like table lounging in chairs that look as if they came off the deck of a fishing boat. The set is in tones of brown and gray. The table turns out to be a finger drawing board for the chairman, who nervously traces designs on its Formica top; the glass of water in front of him announces: "I expect to get a dry mouth because I'll be nervous." The men's suits dissolve into the set; their expressions and messages are equally colorless. After a few minutes, what should have been a stimulating, informative program has turned into a "tranquilizing experience."

I do a great deal of consulting on corporate video and find most often that because those who direct corporate television presentations rarely have had top professional experience, the executive must learn how to protect himself.

Many large corporations are building their own television studios at great expense and hiring their own directors and staff. Unless your company constantly produces messages for its branches via television, it may cost less, and produce better results, to use a professional staff and studio as the need arises. For the cost of one mediocre full-time, and often idle, staff producer and/or director, you can hire first-rate professionals. Ask your local television station for recommendations; directors of documentaries probably are the most appropriate. See samples of their work before you make a commitment.

If you do go outside to hire staff and equipment, you may find that it's more expensive to produce your program at a television studio than it is for the video-makers to come to you. Shooting in a television studio is subject to union regulations calling for a larger crew and longer setting-up time.

No matter who is directing the shooting, or where, and no matter how good the reputation of the studio or director, be prepared to protect yourself. Unfortunately, most staff directors and some outside directors are so in awe of top executives they end up doing them a disservice. They don't suggest or direct enough;

they hesitate to tell the chairman to sit up straight, to tell the legal counsel to take off her dangling earrings.

Here are several keys to self-protection:

Format

The question and answer format or the panel or group discussion is most likely to show you natural and at ease. Those formats give the camera something more than a single speaker on whom to focus. Varied shots—reactions of speakers to one another, for example—relieve monotony. And if you familiarize yourself enough times in rehearsal with the material, you probably can do without a script and/or an accompanying Teleprompter. That will give the program greater spontaneity than set speeches.

You don't need to hire high-priced television personalities to moderate or to conduct the questioning. A personable staff member from your public relations department may do an even better job. That person is more likely to be familiar with the company and may suggest in rehearsal valuable additions to your answers or help to refine the questions.

If you've decided on a "talk to the people" format because you have a lot of information to deliver, pay special attention to your text so that it's in natural, spoken English. A personal story or anecdote as an opening adds warmth and immediacy to your presentation, bringing you closer to your viewers.

The question and answer and panel formats may require little memorization, but they do require rehearsal. Rehearse two or three times and play back the rehearsal on videotape. Your eyes should focus directly on your interviewer. In a panel discussion, your eyes should sweep the other panelists and the moderator. Avoid looking at the ceiling, walls, or floor as you formulate your answer, and don't have long pauses. You know the question, after all. Enough rehearsal will give you smoothness.

If you're delivering a longer talk, the Phrase-a-Line technique described in Chapter 4, well rehearsed, can make you seem warmer and more communicative on the screen.

Teleprompters

A Teleprompter can be a big help in a long speech, but you have to guard against looking dull, with glazed, noncommunicating eyes riveted on it. Teleprompters come in a variety of types and can be rented by the day. The kind most commonly used, in which the script unrolls itself over the eye of the camera, also is the most difficult to work with. It's like trying to talk to a brick wall. As you rehearse, imagine the eyes of a friend beyond the opaque Teleprompter paper and talk into them. Move your head from time to time to avoid that look of Teleprompter rigor mortis. Jim Lehrer on "The MacNeil-Lehrer Report" uses Teleprompter better than almost anyone on TV.

Transparent Teleprompters are more expensive and are not often used except by people addressing large groups. Two Teleprompter screens instead of one are used; as the speaker looks from one to the other for his text, he can give the illusion of eye-sweeping the audience. (If you're speaking in a brightly lighted room, ask to have the lettering reversed; white letters on black make the material easier to read.) It's tricky to get the rhythm of picking up your text from this kind of Teleprompter. (I showed former Vice President Mondale how to do that for his speech at the Democratic National Convention.) With either kind of Teleprompter, plan to rehearse several times with the person who'll be feeding the roll. That way he will get the feel of your pacing, phrasing, and timing, and the roll will move along synchronized smoothly to feed your eyes.

Preparing a Teleprompter script is a meticulous business. The width of the line can be varied—thirty or thirty-two characters is the maximum and lets you pick up at once as many words as possible. Try to get a phrase on a line. If you're using a lectern script as well as a Teleprompter, the two must match exactly. Transferring your script to the Teleprompter roll generally takes the technicians at least three hours; get the material to them early enough. It's for reasons like this that you will need a carefully monitored agenda for rehearsal. Make sure the director understands that you're willing to spend the necessary time.

At his inauguration, President Reagan wisely rejected Teleprompting and instead used large cards on the lectern. Some people prefer to work with four-foot-wide white cue cards, the words printed on them as large as possible with a black felt-tip marker. These are held near the camera in the speaker's line of sight. Picking up your phrases quickly and not staying glued to the cards gives the impression that you're eye-talking.

Don't feel that it's necessary to speak entirely unaided. David Frost spent many successful years as one of the best television talk-show hosts with a clipboard on his lap. Rehearse with whatever helpers you need several times, and play back the videotape to check yourself for eye contact, animation, and pacing—television, as you'll recall, requires pacing a little faster than normal. Check yourself for distracting mannerisms—raising your eyebrows, fidgeting, touching your nose. Contract your vital triangle every time you feel the urge to fidget.

Presenting Yourself Well

Unless you're supremely confident, don't walk while you're talking when the camera is on you. Alvin Perlmutter, Emmy Award-winning producer of documentaries and series including "The Great American Dream Machine" (and the person I picked to produce my own videotapes for teaching corporate executives), advises strongly against walking on the set. It rarely works for nonprofessionals.

If you're using visuals, strive for variety—striking graphics or blocks of different-colored sizes to represent percentages instead of dull black-and-white charts. Your advertising agency can supply you with exciting visuals. Visuals should be on by themselves; don't share the screen with them. Their explanation can be recorded separately—that's called "voice over"—and dubbed onto the tape.

The guidelines for dress and makeup, for pacing, posture, and animation, are the same for corporate TV as they are for commercial television. Don't wear clothes that melt into the set background or fight it. Have a good makeup person and hairdresser in attendance. As Richard Burton has commented: the camera exaggerates. A cowlick or a stray hair or a perspiring chin that might not be noticed in an office can rob you of your viewers' full attention.

Producing Yourself Well

Here's what corporate television producers and directors should take care of for you but too often don't:

THE SET: Corporate television talk-show sets rarely look professional. I've seen so many bad imitations of the MacNeil-Lehrer table that I know you'll do better with a good, solid, round table, about twenty-nine inches high (the top is about elbow height as you're sitting). Tables that are higher and come up to your chest make you look less of an authority. If you're much shorter than anyone else on the screen, ask for a cushion to sit on. A floor-length felt table cover will prevent shots of swinging legs (although there's no excuse for a director to permit such shots).

Surfaces should be clear of any potentials for distraction—pencils, clips, irrelevant papers, and glasses of water invite fingers to fiddle. If you should get dry-mouthed, wait until the camera is off you for a moment and chew your tongue once or twice; that creates saliva.

Straight-backed chairs make you look the most alert and forceful. Kurt Vonnegut once fell asleep on "The David Frost Show" while David was interviewing an evangelist; he might not have if the chair had not been so comfortable. Swivel chairs should be locked. I once saw a distinguished journalist of the New York *Times* swiveling like a whirling dervish. Elizabeth Drew, petite Washington journalist, says, "Chairs ought to come in sizes just as clothes do. I can no more fill out my colleagues' chairs than I can fill out their suits."

For the set background, television blue, a kind of sky blue, is always safe, but dark backgrounds with in-depth lighting are more interesting. Your producer or director should oversee the lighting technicians, but you may have to get into the act. Don't let them highlight your hair at the expense of your face; back-lighting can make a nose look twice as long as it is, and any director who wants to highlight a bald head should have his own head examined. Many corporate television studios have too many overhead lights; you don't need forty. The State Department press briefing room has only eight lights, and they get excellent results. The most flattering lighting is full-face, straight-on lighting. A single spotlight at eye level (it used to be called an "inky-dink") gives a face its best chance.

THE SHOOTING: A good director will aim for a variety of shots —full-face, three-quarter, head-to-waist. A single shot that continues for too long is boring.

Profile shots are unflattering and don't transmit the whole person. If you're bald, close shots can be taken so that the top of your head is cropped just out of the frame of the picture. Shots from below are more flattering than those from above.

Arrange with the director to send you prearranged signals to speed up, slow down, animate, energize. Make it clear to him that you're willing to sit through two or three takes (they can be edited later) in order not to be stuck with a less-than-maximum you.

It's best to shoot in short segments—three to ten minutes—rather than in one long, sustained take. Shorter segments permit immediately prior rehearsal (rehearsing a short segment and then shooting it), which adds to both comfort and spontaneity. Shooting in short segments also can be far less expensive. If a mistake is made, only the segment rather than the entire sequence must be reshot, and short segments cost less to edit.

Corporate television above all should have a spontaneous quality. The people in your worldwide branches should be able to feel your presence even though you're coming to them via television. If you're willing to take the time and effort and to be, when you have to be, your own director, you can send your best self to your viewers instead of a plastic version.

Whether you're on corporate video talking to your own people or on network television talking to the world, whether you're speaking to thousands in an auditorium or to one person at a party, the ability to express yourself with confidence and authority is to your ideas, skills, product, and personality as sunshine is to a stained-glass window. I hope that this book has been illuminating and that it will help you to make the most of your best and the best of all of your communicating situations.

Appendix

Anecdotes and Quotes for Enlivening
  Talks
Drills for Better Speech Sounds
Readings for Practice
Suggested References and Other Aids

ANECDOTES

Anecdotes and quotations make for attention-getting openings, memorable closings, and colorful point-makers throughout your talks (and conversation). Following are some anecdotes clients have used that can be adapted to your uses.

The situation we're facing here reminds me of the time the generator failed in a small town. The city was plunged into darkness and the president of the utility company had tried everything to restore the power and failed. Finally, in despair, he called a professor of engineering from the local college. The fellow walked in, assessed the situation, gave the generator a single tap, and . . . on went the lights!

The professor sent a bill for $1,001 the following day. Puzzled, the president of the utility company called him and said, "I don't understand your bill." The professor replied, "Oh, that's easy: one dollar for tapping, one thousand dollars for knowing *where* to tap."

FOR AN OPENING ADD: We have a major problem in our industry. To find the best solution, we must find out where to "tap." That's what I want to speak with you about today.

FOR A CLOSING ADD: Like the professor, our real value to the industry lies in our know-how . . . and *we know how!* Let's "tap" our resources. Let's make them work for us.

Our situation today is much like that of Oliver Wendell Holmes, who once found himself on a train and couldn't locate his ticket. While the conductor watched, Justice Holmes searched through his pockets in vain. The conductor, who had recognized Holmes, said, "Don't worry, Justice Holmes, you don't need your ticket. You'll probably find it when you get off the train. Just mail it back to the Pennsylvania Railroad." With irritation, the Justice replied, "My dear sir, the problem is *not* 'Where is my ticket?'; the problem is 'Where am I going?' "

FOR AN OPENING ADD: And that is the question haunting Main Street, Wall Street, and Pennsylvania Avenue: "Where are we going?"

FOR A CLOSING ADD: Unlike Justice Holmes, we know where we're going . . . and with your help, we'll get there.

Thomas Edison was mocked for trying unsuccessfully some twelve hundred materials for the filament of his great dream, the incandescent light bulb. "You have failed twelve hundred times," said a regimented thinker of that day. "I have not failed," countered Edison. "I have discovered twelve hundred materials that won't work."

FOR AN OPENING ADD: Like Edison, our company is constantly experimenting and discovering new products . . . that do work. Today I'd like to tell you about some of our most recent and impressive ones.

FOR A CLOSING ADD: We have not failed either. We have succeeded in eliminating all the impossibilities. Now we will succeed in finding the possibilities . . . the answers to our problems.

A mother was having difficulty in waking her son. He pulled the covers over his head. "I'm not going to school," he said. "I'm not ever going to school again." "Are you sick?" his mother asked. "No," he answered, "I'm sick of school. They hate me. They call me names. They make fun of me. Why should I go?" "I can give you two good reasons," the mother replied. "The first is you're forty-two years old, and the second is you're the principal."

FOR AN OPENING ADD: None of us can hide under the covers. We must all face reality . . . the reality of the problem confronting our community.

FOR A CLOSING ADD: We are not going to hide under the covers any longer. Together we will face the problem confronting our community. Together we will win.

The anecdotes below can be used for openings or closings, or sprinkled through the talk to give it flavor.

At a Vikings game a heckler kept shouting his advice to manager Bud Grant. Finally, Bud walked over to the fellow and asked him for his name and business address. Flattered, the heckler asked Grant, "Why do you want to know?" "Because," replied Grant, "I'm going to be at your office early tomorrow morning to tell you how to run *your* business." (Should we be letting Washington tell us how to run our business?)

A friend of mine loves the race track, but one day his luck was terrible. Right before the fourth race, he walked through the paddock and noticed a priest blessing a horse. Sure enough, the horse won easily. In the next race, as my friend watched, the priest mumbled something to another horse who did the same as the first. The next time my friend took down the horse's number, ran to the pari-mutuel window, and put down every last dime he had. And the horse died in the stretch. My friend walked right up to the priest and told him how he'd lost everything. The priest asked, "Are you a Catholic, my son?"
"No, I'm not," my friend said.
"I thought not," replied the priest. "You don't know the difference between giving a blessing and administering last rites." (The super-achievers in this room know the right signs. And there isn't one of you who needs any last rites when it comes to reaching new peaks in sales volume.)

When Oliver Cromwell first coined money under his reign, an adviser noticed that on one side was the inscription "God is with us," and on the other, "The Commonwealth of England." Said the associate, "I see that God and the Commonwealth are on opposite sides." (The economist and the politician need not always be on opposite sides.)

Movie tycoon Samuel Goldwyn's grasp of the English language was less than firm. At one point, Goldwyn became set on having the sharp-tongued intellectual Dorothy Parker come to Hollywood to write for him. His assistant advised against it. "But don't you think she's rather caustic?" the assistant asked. Goldwyn flew into a rage. "What do I care how much she costs? Get her!" (Unfortunately we, unlike Mr. Goldwyn, must consider costs.)

A friend of mine, who was sending her son to camp for the first time, was sent a form to fill out that included the following question: "Is your son a leader or a follower?" One week before camp began, she received a letter that informed her, "The children will meet at 1:00 P.M. There will be seventy-nine leaders and one follower in the group." (You are all leaders . . .)

A South African farmer who had been trying for years to eke out a living from the dry rock soil of his farm finally gave up. He'd heard that people were finding diamonds all over the country, so he sold his farm and set out to look for diamonds.

After a year of fruitless searching, he died penniless and in despair. One day the man to whom he had sold the farm noticed some unusual rocks in a corner of a field. Curious, he took them into his kitchen and washed them off and polished them. That farm turned out to be the first Kimberley diamond mine. (We in this company have untold, unmined diamonds among our products. Let's make sure we don't overlook them.)

Abraham Lincoln ran for Congress in 1846 against Peter Cartwright, a hell-fire-and-damnation evangelist who spread the word that Lincoln was godless. Both candidates attended a revival meeting. "All who desire to give their hearts to God and go to heaven, will stand," shouted Cartwright. Many stood. "All who do not wish to go to hell will stand." Everybody but Lincoln stood. "I observe that everybody but Mr. Lincoln indicated he did not want to go to hell. May I inquire of you, Mr. Lincoln, where are you going?" "Brother Cartwright asks me directly where I am going. I desire to reply with equal directness: I am going to Congress." (I too am sure of one thing—my political candidacy.)

One May Day, as Leonid Brezhnev was reviewing Russia's military might, he kept nodding with approval as the massed infantry divisions marched by, and the thousands of missiles, and the hundreds of tanks. After the tanks came a thin line of twelve gray-haired men dressed in dark blue business suits. Brezhnev's face clouded over. "Are they spies?" asked Brezhnev. "No," replied the head of the Russian armies, "they are economists. You have no idea, Comrade Brezhnev, how much damage twelve economists can do." (Perhaps that story is true. We're not really sure from where the Administration is getting its economic advice these days.)

A teacher herded an unruly child into the principal's office. "This boy," the teacher explained, "is absolutely unmanageable. He is constantly causing trouble in the classroom. He talks back, he—"

"Please," the principal interrupted, "he is only a child. You must show him love, patience, and understanding."

Just then the boy took the principal's inkwell and threw it against the wall, where it splintered and spattered. The principal seized the boy, turned him over his knees, and paddled him until he howled for mercy.

"But you just finished telling me that we must show children patience, love, and understanding!" said the horrified teacher.

"Oh, yes," replied the principal, "but you have to get their attention first." (Getting the attention of our customers . . .)

George Bernard Shaw once sent Winston Churchill an invitation to the opening night of his new play, saying, "Enclosed are two tickets for the first night's performance. Bring a friend—if you have one." Churchill replied, "Thank you very much for the invitation and tickets. Unfortunately, I am busy that night, but could I have tickets for the second night—if there is one?"

A speaker addressing a Welsh audience was carried away by his enthusiasm, and on resuming his seat he apologized to the chairman for having exceeded the time allotted for his speech.

"Oh, no," said the chairman reassuringly, "that was not too long at all. You have merely shortened the winter for us."

Professor Norbert Wiener, a genius of linguistics and philosophy, once was walking down a street near the Massachusetts Institute of Technology, where he taught. A fellow professor, approaching Wiener, detained him for several minutes to ask a question, then excused himself and started off.

"Pardon me a moment, Smith," said Wiener, "but when we stopped to talk, in which direction was I walking?"

Smith smiled at Wiener's confused expression and pointed south. "Why, that way," he said, "toward Massachusetts Avenue."

"Oh, good," Wiener responded, pleased. "In that case, I've already had lunch."

The late Queen Wilhelmina of the Netherlands was noted for her spirit in the international game. During World War I, Kaiser Wilhelm II, dreaming of European conquest, tried to impress her with Germany's strength. "Our guardsmen," he boasted, "are seven feet tall." "And when we open our dikes," the Queen replied quietly, "the waters are ten feet deep."

When James B. Conant was president of Harvard University, he kept among other objects on his desk a statuette of a turtle, on whose base was the inscription: "Consider the turtle. He makes progress only when he sticks his neck out."

After the death of her father, my friend tried to persuade her eighty-year-old mother to move in with her. The older woman was adamant: "No! Absolutely no! I've always said I'd never live with any of my kids. I've seen too many problems arise from that kind of situation."
My friend said, "Yes, Mom, but you're different."
"I know I am," replied her mother, "but you're not."

Lyndon Johnson used to tell a story about patience. "When I was a young Congressman and working with a Senator to get the electric-power people in line, we had a big meeting one night. I lost my temper and told one power man that by God if he didn't do what I wanted to do he could go straight to hell. After the meeting the Senator called me in to his office and said, 'Lyndon, you're a bright young man with a good future. But in twenty seconds you destroyed two months of patient work. Now I'm going to give you some advice, son. It's one thing to tell a man to go to hell, and it's another to make him go there.'"

Dr. George Harris, president of Amherst College, had prepared a long speech to deliver to returning upperclassmen on the day before school began. The welcoming lecture was the only event scheduled that day and the students were restless in their seats as they gazed longingly at the warm autumn sunshine pouring through the windows. Dr. Harris launched into his speech, but after several minutes he himself thought of the golf links.
"I intended to give you some advice," he said, "but I just remembered how much is left over from last year unused." He left the auditorium to thunderous applause.

An Indiana farmer once took his ten-year-old daughter on a trip to the nation's capital so she could see how her government worked. After visiting the House of Representatives, the farmer took his daughter to the gallery of the Senate. As they entered, the chaplain of the Senate was starting to talk.

"Does the chaplain pray for the Senate, Daddy?" asked the little girl.

"No," chuckled the farmer. "He comes in, looks at the Senators, and then prays for the country."

Sometimes it's difficult to see what attracts people to their mates. One couple hired as a maid a conscientious, hard-working woman, but the woman's husband was extremely lazy and lived off her earnings.

The lady of the house was more curious than discreet and finally was unable to restrain herself from asking, "Sarah, why do you put up with him?"

"Well," answered the woman, "it's like this. I make the living, and he makes the living worthwhile."

In his old age, the great French painter Renoir suffered from arthritis. Henri Matisse, his friend, watched sadly as Renoir, grasping a brush with only his fingertips, continued to paint, even though such movement caused stabbing pain.

One day, Matisse asked Renoir why he persisted in painting at the expense of such torture.

Renoir replied, "The pain passes, but the beauty remains."

The only time a person presented an Oscar to himself was when Irving Berlin, opening the Academy Award envelope for the Best Song of 1942, announced: "Irving Berlin for 'White Christmas.'" He did a double take, and then said, "I'm glad to present the award. I've known the fellow for a long time. He's a nice kid and I think he deserves it."

The teacher walked into the noisy classroom, slapped his hand on the desk and ordered sharply: "I demand a little pandemonium!" The class quieted down at once.

"It isn't what you ask for," he announced later in the teachers' lounge. "It's how you ask for it."

At a dinner party in Paris where Benjamin Franklin was one of the distinguished guests, the Abbé Raynal asked, "What kind of man deserves the most pity?" Franklin answered, "A lonesome man on a rainy day who does not know how to read."

Shortly after Harry Thaw, who was convicted of killing architect Stanford White, was released from Sing Sing, he attended the grand opening of the Roxy Theater in New York. As he gazed in horror at the Hollywood-Byzantine lobby, he gasped, "My God, I shot the wrong architect!"

A man was approached by a missionary for a contribution. The man protested that he was in debt, and the missionary said: "Don't you know that you owe more to God than to anyone else?" The man pondered this for a moment and then said, "Yes, but God isn't pressing me."

Whenever Adlai Stevenson noticed children in an audience during his Presidential campaign appearances, he would ask: "How many children would like to be a candidate for the Presidency of the United States?" Almost all the kids would raise their hands. Then Stevenson would ask: "And how many candidates for the Presidency of the United States would like to be children again?" At that point, he would raise his own hand.

Conductor Zubin Mehta once was asked to name his favorite orchestra. He tactfully declined. "What would a devout Muslim answer as to which of his wives he preferred? One can have preferences about details only—a dimple here, an oboe there."

The citizens of a small town in Italy were freed by a soldier of fortune from a foreign oppressor. Daily they debated how to recompense him and concluded that no reward was great enough, not even to make him lord of the city. At last one man said: "Let us kill him and then worship him as our patron saint." And so they did.

A man walked into Johnson's grocery store looking for a bottle of catsup. The shelves of the store were solidly lined with bags of salt— hundreds of them. Mr. Johnson said he had catsup but would have to go down to the cellar to get a bottle. "Say," commented the customer, "you certainly must sell a lot of salt in this store!" "Nope," said Mr. Johnson with resignation. "I can't sell salt hardly at all. But the fellow who sells *me* salt—can *he* sell salt!"

Danny Kaye was playing golf with a famous lawyer, Frank Weil. Frank's shot off the first tee went about twenty feet into the rough. He took out a number-three wood and hit the ball right to the green, where it landed six inches from the cup. "You always were great on appeal, Frank," Danny said.

George Bernard Shaw once was invited to speak at a seminar. The presentations were far too many and far too long. The audience waited expectantly for Shaw, who was the last to speak. When the roar of applause had subsided, he said, "Ladies and gentlemen, the subject is not exhausted, but we are," and sat down.

QUOTES

Action

If you can't do, be around people who do do.

—ERMA BOMBECK

Advice

By the time a man asks you for advice, he has generally made up his mind what he wants to do, and is looking for confirmation rather than counseling.

—SYDNEY J. HARRIS

The art of giving advice is to make the recipient believe he thought of it himself.

—FRANK TYGER

Age

If you wish to live long you must be willing to grow old.

—GEORGE LAWTON

Middle age is when your clothes no longer fit, and it's you who need the alterations.

—EARL WILSON

Growing old is no more than a bad habit which a busy man has no time to form.

—ANDRÉ MAUROIS

To me, old age is fifteen years older than I am.

—BERNARD M. BARUCH

Alone

Alone is not so bad if together is not so good.

—LOLA FALANA

Appreciation

The deepest principle in human nature is the craving to be appreciated.

—WILLIAM JAMES

When people are made to feel secure and important and appreciated, it will no longer be necessary for them to whittle down others in order to seem bigger by comparison.

—VIRGINIA ARCASTLE

Automation

Machines are beneficial to the degree that they eliminate the need for labor, harmful to the degree that they eliminate the need for skill.

—W. H. AUDEN

Automation is a technological process that does all the work while you just sit there. When you were younger, this was called "Mother."

—ANONYMOUS

Bore

A bore is a man who deprives you of solitude without providing you with company.

—GIAN VINCENZO GRAVIN

A bore—someone who persists in holding to his own views after we have enlightened him with ours.

—MALCOLM FORBES

Bosses

I've come to this conclusion,
It's one I've long supposed;
The boss's door is open—
It's his mind that's always closed.

—ROBERT ORBEN

Brains

The brain is a wonderful organ; it starts working the moment you get up in the morning, and does not stop until you get into the office.

—ROBERT LEE FROST

Brevity

There is much to be said for not saying much.

—FRANK TYGER

Change

Change, not habit, is what gets most of us down; habit is the stabilizer of human society, change accounts for its progress.

—WILLIAM FEATHER

There is danger in reckless change, but greater danger in blind conservatism.

—HENRY GEORGE

Character

How a man plays the game shows something of his character; how he loses shows all of it.

—CAMDEN COUNTY, GEORGIA, *Tribune*

Not merely what we do, but what we try to do and why, are the true interpreters of what we are.

—C. H. WOODARD

Children

It's easy to understand the truth of the recent report that says children of today behave worse than children of a generation ago. It's primarily because those weren't children—they were us.

—*Weight Watchers Magazine*

It sometimes happens, even in the best of families, that a baby is born. This is not necessarily a cause for alarm. The important thing is to keep your wits about you and borrow some money.

—ELINOR GOULDING SMITH

Choice

We inherit our relatives and our features and may not escape them; but we can select our clothing and our friends, and let us be careful that both fit us.

—VOLNEY STREAMER

Conceit

Conceit is the quicksand of success.

—ARNOLD GLASOW

Conversation

Nothing lowers the level of conversation more than raising the voice.

—STANLEY HOROWITZ

The world would be happier if men had the same capacity to be silent that they have to speak.

—BARUCH SPINOZA

I don't care how much a man talks, if he only says it in a few words.

—JOSH BILLINGS

Courage

Act with a determination not to be turned aside by thoughts of the past and fears of the future.

—ROBERT E. LEE

Don't be afraid to take a big step if one is indicated. You can't cross a chasm in two small jumps.

—DAVID LLOYD GEORGE

Creativity

Iron rusts from disuse; water loses its purity from stagnation and in cold weather becomes frozen; even so does inaction sap the vigors of the mind.

—LEONARDO DA VINCI

Benjamin Franklin may have discovered electricity—but it was the man who invented the meter who made the money.

—Quoted by EARL WILSON

Culture

One ought at least to hear a little melody every day, read a fine poem, see a good picture, and, if possible, make a few sensible remarks.

—GOETHE

Decision-making

When the assistant football coach was made head coach, he was asked how he felt. He said, "I'm learning the difference between making recommendations and making decisions."

—ANONYMOUS

Democracy

Many Americans cannot define democracy; they are much like the schoolboy who, when he was asked to define an elephant, confessed he was unable to do so but insisted he would recognize an elephant when he saw one.

—ADLAI STEVENSON

Difficulties

It is not because things are difficult that we do not dare; it is because we do not dare that they are difficult.

—SENECA

Discipline

No steam or gas ever drives anything until it is confined. No Niagara is ever turned into light and power until it is tunneled. No life ever grows until it is focused, dedicated, disciplined.

—HARRY EMERSON FOSDICK

Duty

It's not enough that we do our best; sometimes we have to do what's required.

—WINSTON CHURCHILL

I am only one, but still I am one. I cannot do everything, but still I can do something, and because I cannot do everything, I will not refuse to do the something that I can do.

—EDWARD EVERETT HALE

Education

Two delusions fostered by higher education are that what is taught corresponds to what is learned, and that it will somehow pay off in money.

—WILLIAM FEATHER

Education is the ability to listen to almost anything without losing your temper or your self-confidence.

—ROBERT FROST

Enthusiasm

Dirty ore wrought in white-heat enthusiasm can be transformed into shining steel. Enthusiasm is the electric current that keeps the engine of life going at top speed. Enthusiasm is the very propeller of progress. All great achievements have sprung from the fount of enthusiasm. Search and you will find that at the base and birth of every great business organization is an enthusiast, a man consumed with earnestness of purpose, with confidence in his powers, with faith in the worthwhileness of his endeavors.

—B. C. FORBES

Example

Example is not the main thing in influencing others. It is the only thing.

—ALBERT SCHWEITZER

Failure

When you are down and out, something always turns up—and it is usually the noses of your friends.

—ORSON WELLES

Faith

You must not lose faith in humanity. Humanity is an ocean; if a few drops of the ocean are dirty, the ocean does not become dirty.

—MAHATMA GANDHI

Flattery

A compliment is baloney sliced so thin it's delectable. Flattery is baloney sliced so thick it's indigestible.

—ARCHBISHOP FULTON J. SHEEN

Freedom

If a nation values anything more than freedom, it will lose its freedom, and the irony of it is that if it is comfort or money that it values more, it will lose that too.

—SOMERSET MAUGHAM

Those who expect to reap the blessing of freedom must undertake to support it.

—THOMAS PAINE

Remember, as once it was said: "When the freedom they wished for most was freedom from responsibility, then Athens ceased to be free."

—HENRY A. BRUINSMA

Friendship

You can make more friends in two months by becoming really interested in other people, than you can in two years by trying to get other people interested in you.

—DALE CARNEGIE

Hunt for the good in the other fellow—he has to do the same in your case.

—WILLIAM FEATHER

You must look into people, as well as at them.

—LORD CHESTERFIELD

Future

I don't know who my grandfather was; I am much more concerned to know what his grandson will be.

—ABRAHAM LINCOLN

Real generosity toward the future consists in giving all to what is present.

—ALBERT CAMUS

Giving

You may give gifts without caring, but you can't care without giving.

—FRANK A. CLARK

Only a life lived for others is a life worthwhile.

—ALBERT EINSTEIN

The making of money, the accumulation of material power, is not all there is to living. Life is something more than these, and the man who misses this truth misses the greatest joy and satisfaction that can come into his life—service for others.

—EDWARD BOK

Goals

Being easy-going when you have a goal to reach seldom makes the going easy.

—FRANK TYGER

The way to gain a good reputation is to endeavor to be what you desire to appear.

—SOCRATES

In life, as in football, you won't go far unless you know where the goalposts are.

—ARNOLD GLASOW

Government

A government that provides total security for its people, foresees and supplies their necessities, manages their principal concerns, directs their industry, regulates the descent of property and subdivides their inheritance—what remains but to spare them all the care of thinking, and all the trouble of living.

—ALEXIS DE TOCQUEVILLE

The punishment of wise men who refuse to take part in the affairs of government is to live under the government of unwise men.

—PLATO

Happiness

Happiness is a by-product of an effort to make someone else happy.

—GRETA PALMER

Human Nature

It is human nature to think wisely and act foolishly.

—ANATOLE FRANCE

Humility

Plenty of people want to be pious, but no one wants to be humble.

—LA ROCHEFOUCAULD

When a man realizes his littleness, his greatness can appear.

—H. G. WELLS

Humor

A touch of folly is needed if we are to extricate ourselves successfully from some of the hazards of life.

—LA ROCHEFOUCAULD

Men show their character in nothing more clearly than by what they think laughable.

—GOETHE

Idealism

An idealist is one who, on noticing that a rose smells better than a cabbage, concludes that it will also make better soup.

—H. L. MENCKEN

Ideals

We all must have ideals unless we are content to drift along aimlessly, ambitionless, ineffectually. Ideals vitalize. Ideals energize.

—B. C. FORBES

Idleness

Idleness is the burial of a living man.

—Jeremy Taylor

It is impossible to enjoy idling thoroughly unless one has plenty of work to do.

—Jerome K. Jerome

Even if you're on the right track, you'll get run over if you just sit there.

—Will Rogers

Imagination

When I was younger I could remember anything, whether it had happened or not.

—Mark Twain

Inventors

An inventor is an engineer who doesn't take his education too seriously.

—Charles Kettering

Jogging

America is the only country in the world where people jog ten miles a day for exercise and then take an elevator up to the mezzanine.

—Robert Orben

Judgment

We judge ourselves by what we feel capable of doing, while others judge us by what we have already done.

—Henry Wadsworth Longfellow

Not all things have to be scrutinized, nor all friends tested, nor all enemies exposed and denounced.

—Spanish proverb

Kindness

A little kindness from person to person is better than a vast love for all humankind.

—Richard Dehmel

Kindness is a language which the deaf can hear and the blind can read.

—MARK TWAIN

Knowledge

To be conscious that you are ignorant is a great step to knowledge.

—BENJAMIN DISRAELI

Doubt is the key to knowledge.

—PERSIAN PROVERB

Knowledge is the antidote to fear.

—RALPH WALDO EMERSON

Laws

The less people know about how sausages and laws are made, the better they will sleep at night.

—OTTO VON BISMARCK

We are in bondage to the law in order that we may be free.

—CICERO

Laws are spider webs through which the big flies pass and the little ones get caught.

—HONORÉ DE BALZAC

Leadership

Leadership is the ability to get men to do what they don't want to do and like it.

—HARRY S TRUMAN

I've got to follow them. I am their leader.

—ALEXANDRE LEDRU-ROLLIN

Learning

I find that a great part of the information I have was acquired by looking up something and finding something else on the way.

—FRANKLIN P. ADAMS

The man who is too old to learn was probably always too old to learn.

—ANONYMOUS

Leisure

The busiest men have the most leisure.

—ENGLISH PROVERB

The real problem of leisure time is how to keep others from using yours.

—ARTHUR LACEY

Life

Life is too short to be little.

—BENJAMIN DISRAELI

Life is really simple, but we insist on making it complicated.

—CONFUCIUS

Life is like a game of poker; if you don't put any in the pot, there won't be any to take out.

—MOMS MABLEY

Every twenty-four hours, the world turns over on someone who was sitting on top of it.

—HUGH ALLEN

With most men life is like backgammon—half skill and half luck.

—OLIVER WENDELL HOLMES

Living

When we are young, we are slavishly employed in procuring something whereby we may live comfortably when we grow old; and when we are old, we perceive it is too late to live as we proposed.

—ALEXANDER POPE

When it is time to die, let us not discover that we have never lived.

—HENRY DAVID THOREAU

Love

Love and a cough cannot be hid.

—GEORGE HERBERT

To feed men and not to love them is to treat them as if they were barnyard cattle. To love them and not to respect them is to treat them as if they were household pets.

—MENCIUS

Platonic love is love from the neck up.

—THYRA SAMTER WINSLOW

Management

Management by objectives works if you know the objectives. Ninety percent of the time you don't.

—PETER DRUCKER

Marriage

My marriage was the most fortunate and joyous event which happened to me in the whole of my life, for what can be more glorious than to be united in one's walk through life with a being incapable of an ignoble thought.

—WINSTON CHURCHILL

The most important thing a father can do for his children is to love their mother.

—THEODORE HESBURGH

Maturity

You are not mature until you expect the unexpected.

—CHICAGO *Tribune*

Maturity: Among other things, not to hide one's strength out of fear and, consequently, live below one's best.

—DAG HAMMARSKJÖLD

Mind

Minds are like parachutes. They only function when open.

—JAMES DEWAR

Vacant lots and vacant minds attract the most rubbish.

—ARNOLD GLASOW

There is nothing so elastic as the human mind. The more we are obliged to do, the more we are able to accomplish.

—TRYON EDWARDS

Miracles

Anyone who doesn't believe in miracles is not a realist.

—DAVID BEN GURION

Mistakes

He who never made a mistake never made a discovery.

—SAMUEL SMILES

A man who has committed a mistake and doesn't correct it is committing another mistake.

—CONFUCIUS

I have lived in this world just long enough to look carefully the second time into things that I am the most certain of the first time.

—JOSH BILLINGS

Only some of us can learn by other people's mistakes. The rest of us have to be the other people.

—CHICAGO *Tribune*

Money

If you would know the value of money, go and try to borrow some.

—BENJAMIN FRANKLIN

Make money your God, it will plague you like the devil.

—HENRY FIELDING

In some ways, a millionaire just can't win. If he spends too freely, he is criticized for being extravagant and ostentatious. If, on the other hand, he lives quietly and thriftily, the same people who would have criticized him for being profligate will call him a miser.

—J. PAUL GETTY

Civilization and profits go hand in hand.

—CALVIN COOLIDGE

Viewing the matter in retrospect, I can testify that it is nearly always easier to make one million dollars honestly than to dispose of it wisely.

—JULIUS ROSENWALD

Music

I love playing the violin, especially when I am depressed; it helps me keep my chin up.

—ANONYMOUS

Many people would like to see two groups stand on their records— politicians and rock musicians.

Modern Maturity magazine

Nonconformists

Nonconformists travel as a rule in bunches. You rarely find a nonconformist who goes it alone. And woe to him inside a nonconformist clique who does not conform with nonconformity.

—ERIC HOFFER

Obstacles

If you find a path with no obstacles, it probably doesn't lead anywhere.

—FRANK A. CLARK

History has demonstrated that the most notable winners usually encountered heartbreaking obstacles before they triumphed. They finally won because they refused to become discouraged by their defeats. Disappointments acted as a challenge. Don't let difficulties discourage you.

—B. C. FORBES

The block of granite which was an obstacle in the pathway of the weak becomes a stepping-stone in the pathway of the strong.

—THOMAS CARLYLE

Opinions

We probably wouldn't worry about what people think of us if we could know how seldom they do.

—OLIN MILLER

If in the last few years you hadn't discarded a major opinion or acquired a new one, check your pulse. You may be dead.

—GELETT BURGESS

If fifty million people say a foolish thing, it is still a foolish thing.

—ANATOLE FRANCE

Opportunity

The lure of the distant and the difficult is deceptive. The great opportunity is where you are.

—JOHN BURROUGHS

Opportunity seems to knock some people cold.

—WILLIAM FEATHER

Opportunity can be spelled with four letters. But these letters are not L-U-CK. They are W-O-R-K.

—B. C. FORBES

Optimism

I am an optimist. It does not seem too much use being anything else.
—WINSTON CHURCHILL

Some people are always grumbling that roses have thorns: I am thankful that thorns have roses.
—ALPHONSE KARR

I make the most of all that comes, and the least of all that goes.
—SARA TEASDALE

Parents

Any kid who has two parents who are interested in him and has a houseful of books isn't poor.
—SAM LEVENSON

Some parents give most by giving least.
—ARNOLD GLASOW

Patience

Patience: A minor form of despair, disguised as a virtue.
—AMBROSE BIERCE

If you are patient in one moment of anger, you will escape a hundred days of sorrow.
—CHINESE PROVERB

Patience is bitter, but its fruits are sweet.
—JEAN JACQUES ROUSSEAU

Whether it's marriage or business, patience is the first rule of success.
—WILLIAM FEATHER

Perceptions

We do not see things as they are, we see things as we are.
—THE TALMUD

Perseverance

Perseverance is failing nineteen times and succeeding the twentieth.
—J. ANDREWS

Diamonds are chunks of coal that stuck to their job.
—B. C. FORBES

Persuasion

One of the best ways to persuade others is with your ears—by listening to them.

—DEAN RUSK

Pessimism

An optimist sees an opportunity in every calamity; a pessimist sees a calamity in every opportunity.

—WINSTON CHURCHILL

Pessimism in our time is infinitely more respectable than optimism; the man who foresees peace, prosperity, and a decline in juvenile delinquency is a negligent and vacuous fellow. The man who forsees catastrophe has a gift of insight which insures that he will become a radio commentator, an editor of *Time,* or go to Congress.

—JOHN KENNETH GALBRAITH

Pleasures

Do not bite at the bait of pleasure till you know there is no hook beneath it.

—THOMAS JEFFERSON

The liberty of using harmless pleasure will not be disputed; but it is still to be examined what pleasures are harmless.

—SAMUEL JOHNSON

Politics

As any smart politician knows, the best position to take is one that's to the left of the Republicans, to the right of the Democrats, and to the front of the cameras.

—ROBERT ORBEN

What is politics but persuading the public to vote for this and support that and endure these for the promise of those?

—GILBERT HIGHET

In politics, merit is rewarded by the possessor being raised, like a target, to a position to be fired at.

—CHRISTIAN BOVEE

Every time we have an election, we get in worse men and the country keeps right on going. Times have proven only one good thing and that is you can't ruin this country even with politics.

—WILL ROGERS

The cheapest way to have your family tree traced is to run for office.

—ARNOLD GLASOW

Pollution

Some poets now envision the world ending with neither a bang nor a whimper, but with a hacking cough.

—ANONYMOUS

I'm not saying our beaches are polluted, but when you pick up a shell to hear the sea, it leaves a ring around your ear.

—DICK CAVETT

Power

Nearly all men can stand adversity, but if you want to test a man's character, give him power.

—ABRAHAM LINCOLN

Praise

People ask you for criticism, but they only want praise.

—SOMERSET MAUGHAM

Reprove privately, praise publicly.

—ARNOLD GLASOW

Prejudices

A great number of people think they are thinking when they are merely rearranging their prejudices.

—WILLIAM JAMES

Everyone is a prisoner of his own experiences. No one can eliminate prejudices—just recognize them.

—EDWARD R. MURROW

Pride

Pride is at the bottom of all great mistakes.

—JOHN RUSKIN

There is this paradox in pride—it makes some men ridiculous, but prevents others from becoming so.

—CHARLES CALEB COLTON

Progress

Progress always involves risks. You can't steal second base and keep your foot on first.

—FREDERICK WILCOX

Progress is wonderful. Now you can send a letter from one city to another and the post office promises you next day delivery. It costs $7.50 and it's called Express Mail. I can remember when it cost 3¢ and it was called U.S. mail.

—ROBERT ORBEN

I know there are utopians who believe that human progress is inevitable, a divine trajectory irreversible in its upward motion. Let me just point out to them that in the last few thousand years we have blazed what I consider to be a trail of questionable glory—from Abraham and Isaac to Dennis the Menace.

—ADLAI E. STEVENSON

Progress is not created by contented people.

—FRANK TYGER

Public Speaking

The best after-dinner speech I ever heard was "May I have the check, please?"

—BERNARD MELTZER

It's never easy to be a substitute speaker. The audience always looks on you the same way they look on making out their income tax. They hope for the best but they're prepared for the worst.

—ROBERT ORBEN

Religion

Going to church doesn't make a man a Christian any more than going into a garage makes a man an automobile.

—BILLY SUNDAY

Religion is a candle inside a multicolored lantern. Everyone looks through a particular color, but the candle is always there.

—MOHAMMED NAGUIB

Reputation

You can't build a reputation on what you are going to do.

—HENRY FORD

If you are standing upright, don't worry if your shadow is crooked.
—CHINESE PROVERB

Resolution

Every human mind is a great slumbering power until awakened by keen desire and by definite resolution to do.
—EDGAR F. ROBERTS

The man with the average mentality, but with control, with a definite goal, and a clear conception of how it can be gained, and above all, with the power of application and labor, wins in the end.
—WILLIAM HOWARD TAFT

Respect

What people say behind your back is your standing in the community in which you live.

—E. W. HOWE

The respect of those you respect is worth more than the applause of the multitude.

—ARNOLD GLASOW

Responsibility

Let everyone sweep in front of his own door and the whole world will be clean.

—GOETHE

Responsibility is the thing people dread most of all. Yet it is the one thing in the world that develops us, gives us manhood or womanhood fiber.

—FRANK CRANE

Retirement

Retired is being tired twice—first, tired of working; then, tired of not.
—ROSE L. SANDS

Don't think of retiring from the world until the world will be sorry that you retire.

—ANONYMOUS

Rights

Among the most precious rights of man is the right to be wrong.
—FRANK TYGER

I do not say that all men are equal in their ability, character, and motivation, I do say that every American should be given a fair chance to develop all the talents he may have.

—JOHN F. KENNEDY

Risk

The policy of being too cautious is the greatest risk of all.

—JAWAHARLAL NEHRU

You can't just go on being a good egg. You must either hatch or go bad!

—C. S. LEWIS

The word impossible is not in my dictionary.

—NAPOLEON BONAPARTE

Mankind would be vastly poorer if it had not been for men who were willing to take risks against the longest odds. Even if it could be done, we would be foolish to try to stamp out this willingness in man to buck seemingly hopeless odds. Our problem is how to remain properly venturesome and experimental without making fools of ourselves.

—BERNARD BARUCH

Rumors

Rumors without a leg to stand on still have a way of getting around.

—CHICAGO *Tribune*

Salesmen

The most important part of being a salesman is confidence. Confidence is going after Moby Dick with a rowboat, a harpoon, and a jar of tartar sauce.

—ROBERT ORBEN

Savings

Nowadays the birds are the only creatures who have nest eggs.

—W. F. DETTLE

Self-control

The man who would control others must be able to control himself.

—B. C. FORBES

He who gains a victory over other men is strong, but he who gains a victory over himself is all-powerful.

—LAO-TZU

Self-pity

Rebellion against your handicaps gets you nowhere. Self-pity gets you nowhere. One must have the adventurous daring to accept oneself as a bundle of possibilities and undertake the most interesting game in the world—making the most of one's best.

—HARRY EMERSON FOSDICK

Silence

Better silent than stupid.

—GERMAN PROVERB

If you don't say anything, you won't be called on to repeat it.

—CALVIN COOLIDGE

Sin

One of the Apostles said that the wages of sin is death. The price hasn't been reduced.

—DAVID OGILVY

Adam ate the apple, and our teeth still ache.

—HUNGARIAN PROVERB

God may forgive you your sins, but your nervous system won't.

—ALFRED KORZYBSKI

Solutions

"I must do something" will always solve more problems than "something must be done."

—*Bits & Pieces*

It is a common experience that a problem difficult at night is resolved in the morning after the committee of sleep has worked on it.

—JOHN STEINBECK

Sorrow

We have no right to ask when sorrow comes, "Why did this happen to me?" unless we ask the same question for every joy that comes our way.

—PHILIP S. BERNSTEIN

Sorrow is like a precious treasure, shown only to friends.

—AFRICAN PROVERB

Speaking up

The hottest places in Hell are reserved for those who, in a period of moral crisis, maintain their neutrality.

—DANTE

Statesmanship

A statesman is a politician who's been dead ten or fifteen years.

—HARRY S TRUMAN

Strength

Some people think it's holding on that makes one strong. Sometimes it's letting go.

—SYLVIA ROBINSON

Success

Success is a journey—not a destination.

—H. TOM COLLARD

I never did anything worth doing by accident, nor did any of my inventions come by accident; they came by work.

—THOMAS A. EDISON

Coming together is a beginning; keeping together is progress; working together is success.

—HENRY FORD

For success, attitude is equally as important as ability.

—HARRY F. BANKS

Tact

Tact is the knack of making a point without making an enemy.

—HOWARD W. NEWTON

Talent

We are told that talent creates its own opportunities. But it sometimes seems that intense desire creates not only its own opportunities, but its own talents.

—ERIC HOFFER

One of the greatest talents of all is the talent to recognize and to develop talent in others.

—FRANK TYGER

Taxes

Next to being shot at and missed, nothing is really quite as satisfying as an income tax refund.
—F. J. RAYMOND

The thing generally raised on city land is taxes.
—CHARLES DUDLEY WARNER

We're taxed right and left. Report our taxes right and we have nothing left.
—ARNOLD GLASOW

I like to pay taxes. With them I buy civilization.
—OLIVER WENDELL HOLMES

Teaching

There is nothing more inspiring than having a mind unfold before you. Let people teach who have a calling. It is never just a job.
—ABRAHAM KAPLAN

The art of being taught is the art of discovery, as the art of teaching is the art of assisting discovery to take place.
—MARK VAN DOREN

Technology

Man has mounted science, and is now run away with. I firmly believe that before many centuries more, science will be the master of man. The engines he will have invented will be beyond his strength to control. Some day science may have the existence of mankind in its power, and the human race may commit suicide by blowing up the world.
—HENRY ADAMS (1862)

Temper

Temper, if ungoverned, governs the whole man.
—ANTHONY SHAFTESBURY

A tart temper never mellows with age, and a sharp tongue is the only edged tool that grows keener with constant use.
—WASHINGTON IRVING

Tennis

Never fall in love with a tennis player. To him, love means nothing.
—ANONYMOUS

Thinking

In order to acquire intellect one must need it. One loses it when it is no longer necessary.

—FRIEDRICH NIETZSCHE

To read without reflecting is like eating without digesting.

—EDMUND BURKE

What is the hardest task in the world? To think.

—RALPH WALDO EMERSON

If you make people think they're thinking, they'll love you; but if you really make them think, they'll hate you.

—DON MARQUIS

Time

Without the management of time, you will soon have nothing left to manage.

—WILLIAM D. REIFF

You will never *find* time for anything. If you want time, you must make it.

—CHARLES BUXTON

Trouble

Never bear more than one kind of trouble at a time. Some people bear three—all they have had, all they have now, and all they expect to have.

—EDWARD EVERETT HALE

When I go to bed, I leave my troubles in my clothes.

—DUTCH PROVERB

Truth

Truth is so hard to tell, it sometimes needs fiction to make it plausible.

—DAGOBERT D. RUNES

He who would speak the truth must have one foot in the stirrup.

—TURKISH PROVERB

Every man has a right to utter what he thinks truth, and every other man has a right to knock him down for it.

—SAMUEL JOHNSON

Values

The society which scorns excellence in plumbing because plumbing is a humble activity and tolerates shoddiness in philosophy because it is an exalted activity will have neither good plumbing nor good philosophy. Neither its pipes nor its theories will hold water.

—JOHN W. GARDNER

Virtue

Wisdom is knowing what to do next, virtue is doing it.

—DAVID STARR JORDAN

War

I wonder what our world would be like if men always had sacrificed as freely to prevent wars as to win them.

—FRANK A. CLARK

There is no such thing as an inevitable war. If war comes it will be from failure of human wisdom.

—BONAR LAW

Wealth

Wealth is a means to an end, not the end itself. As a synonym for health and happiness, it has had a fair trial and failed dismally.

—JOHN GALSWORTHY

Superfluous wealth can buy superfluities only.

—HENRY DAVID THOREAU

Will

Where the willingness is great, the difficulties cannot be great.

—NICCOLÒ MACHIAVELLI

Winning

Winning isn't everything, but losing isn't anything.

—VINCE LOMBARDI

Wisdom

A man begins cutting his wisdom teeth the first time he bites off more than he can chew.

—HERB CAEN

Where wisdom is called for, force is of little use.

—HERODOTUS

We should be careful to get out of an experience all the wisdom that is in it, like the cat that sits down on a hot stove lid. She will never sit down on a hot stove lid again. But she will never again sit down on a cold one either.

—MARK TWAIN

Nine-tenths of wisdom consists in being wise in time.

—THEODORE ROOSEVELT

Work

Work is what you do when you'd rather be doing something else.

—ANONYMOUS

No man needs sympathy because he has to work. Far and away the best prize that life offers is the chance to work hard at work worth doing.

—THEODORE ROOSEVELT

Delegating work works, provided the one delegating works too.

—ROBERT HALF

The trouble with today's work-less philosophies is that they don't work.

—ARNOLD GLASOW

Worry

As a cure for worrying, work is better than whiskey.

—THOMAS A. EDISON

Elephants live longer than people, according to a book we read. Maybe that's because they never worry about trying to lose weight.

—COUNCIL BLUFFS, IOWA, *Nonpareil*

Drills for Better Speech Sounds

LACK OF PROJECTION AND WHISPER TALKING

Do people constantly ask you to repeat what you said? To recognize whisper talk, put a finger against your Adam's apple and say, "zzzzz." You feel a vibration; "zzzzz" cannot be said in a true whisper; it is a voiced tone. Now say, "sssss." Your larynx does not vibrate. "Ssssss" is the unvoiced whispered counterpart of "zzzzz."

Now place your finger on your larynx and say in your normal voice, "I wonder whether I'll feel a vibration." If the buzz is missing, you are a whisper speaker.

Do not confuse whisper speaking with soft but supported speaking, nor with a stage whisper. The stage whisper is supported by almost as much air pressure as a declamation. In the theater, it can be heard in the farthest row of the balcony. The unprojected speaker, by contrast, is almost inaudible. Jacqueline Kennedy Onassis is a breathy, whisper speaker.

Lack of breath support may show itself not only in whispering but in strain. If your throat tires quickly when you talk, if you constantly clear it, if you are chronically hoarse though you haven't a cold, don't smoke, and have been told by your doctor that there is nothing organically wrong with your throat, you are not supporting your voice. The result is likely to be a fuzzy, foggy, grating sound that irritates the listener's throat as well as your own.

For better projection, do the following exercises (and those on page 20) four or five times a day. Do the exercises standing, chest up, stomach in. Do not take a deep breath.

1. Numbers. Take a short sip of breath and count aloud on a long single exhalation as fast as you can. The first time try for forty. This is the only time you will be permitted to mumble, so take advantage of it. We are not concerned here with the sound you make, but only with your breath support. Each day, go a little further. Shoot for 120.

2. The Puncher. Locate your vital triangle once more. Now start to count aloud, preceding each number with a light grunt and punching the number: "Uh-*one!* Uh-*two!* Uh-*three!*" Emphasize the numbers, not the grunt. Don't separate the "uh" from the numbers; connect them. With no break in your breath, dig into each number, trying to boom like a big bass drum. You will find your breath support seems to go right down to your groin.

3. Round and Round. Standing chest up, stomach in, describe full, rich vocal circles on

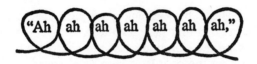

with unbroken supported sound, while you make circles with your hands for your eye to see. As each sound hits the bottom of its circle, give it renewed energy by pulling in your vital triangle muscles, giving the sound a new thrust of energy. You should sound like a record with a needle stuck in a groove. The sound rolls over and over. Try the exercise on "wah, wah, wah," "waw, waw, waw," "woh, woh, woh." Remember to give each circle of sound a new push with your vital triangle muscles. Dig down, down, down in pitch and support, as though you were digging for a new low in voice range. Pretend your lips are down where your navel is, that you had to go all the way down there to get your voice. Don't start your voice at your neck or collarbone.

4. Breath Massage. The above exercises for supporting the voice will help you avoid strain. Clearing the throat, harumphing, abuses the vocal cords and can make you hoarse. Should you have any sign of hoarseness, give your vocal cords this breath massage:

You've seen a dog stretched out on a rug, his jaw loose, his tongue hanging limply as he pants. Imitate the dog's panting, but first yawn until you feel an open throat. With mouth lax and tongue limp, pant low and slow in your throat. With mouth lax and tongue limp, inhale and exhale audibly but smoothly over the floor of your mouth. In and out, in and out. Feel the cool air moving over the tongue, down the windpipe and then back up again. Feel the air brushing and blowing the phlegm off your vocal cords. This exercise tends to dry the throat, so breathe this way seven or eight times and then swallow. Repeat the process ten times. Rest and repeat an hour later if necessary. Breathe audibly, in and out, sounding like an old-fashioned steam locomotive puffing and idling in the station.

If there really is something the matter with your throat, though, you don't need speech exercises, you need a throat specialist. If you have acute laryngitis, he will tell you to stop talking and even to stop whispering. Smoking also is out.

To avoid laryngitis, speak as little as possible whenever a serious cold goes from your nose to your throat or chest. If you strain your voice at that point, you invite polyps or nodes.

NASALITY AND STRIDENCY

Close your nostrils by clasping your nose between thumb and forefinger. Then say, "Mimi sang seventeen songs and swooned." Your fingers will pick up the vibration caused in your nose by the "m," "n," and "ng." These are the only legitimate nasal sounds in our language.

Now close your nostrils again and say, "Woe, oh woe, oh woe." If you buzz at all, you are a nose talker. An actor who wants to project a complaining and disagreeable character often adopts a nasal speech pattern.

You cannot be attractive if you talk through your nose. You will be whining, naggy, negative. Your voice comes out through your nose if your mouth does not open enough when you talk. Look into your mirror and say, "Hi, you wonderful, lovable creature." Throughout a good part of that sentence there should be almost a half-inch strip of darkness between your teeth. If, instead, your teeth are fitted together like two rows of corn on the cob or, even worse, if your lips are virtually closed like those of a ventriloquist, you almost certainly speak nasally.

Stridency and shrillness are even more disagreeable than nasality. Look at yourself in a mirror as you talk. Does your neck look taut? Do the veins and cords stand out like ropes? Are the muscles around your chin tight to the eye and the touch? If they are, you probably sound screechy. Tie a ribbon snugly around your neck and talk. If you strain or force your voice, you will feel the ribbon choking you.

To correct both nasality and stridency, and instead have the velvet smoothness of chest resonance, learn to relax your jaw and tongue and open your mouth so that the sound exits that way.

I cannot remove the causes of your tension, but at least I can help you get rid of some of the effects. These anti-nasality exercises also will relax you all over. For more Stress Breakers, see Chapter 7.

1. The Ventriloquist. To know how far your jaw can relax, first put your fingertips in front of your ears, at the spot where your lower and upper jaw are hinged together. With your mouth closed, the place is a slight bump. As you drop your jaw, the bump will go away and be replaced by a cavity. Watch yourself in the mirror. Relaxed enough, your lower jaw will drop behind the upper one. Don't worry about the row of double chins; they will disappear when these maneuvers are over. (Stridency, shrillness, and nasality soon will vanish too.) Place your index finger against your chin and manipulate your lower jaw until it stops fighting you and swings freely. It should be as loose as a ventriloquist's dummy's. With jaws clenched and lips drawn, you are more like the ventriloquist.

2. The Groaner. Tuck your tongue between your lower lip and your teeth, relaxed and thick. Now groan "Aaaaaah," dragging out the sound and directing it at the point where your tongue and lip meet. You will have the sensation that the "Aaaaaah" is actually outside your mouth—which is exactly where it should be.

3. Tongue Talk. If I ask you to let your head sag on your neck, you will have no trouble doing that. But can you relax your tongue? In a mirror, check: Can you let it go limp, completely without tension, resting sleepily in the nest of the floor of your mouth? Most people cannot. Your tongue probably will hump up, furrow, pull back, stretch sideways. Talk to it as if to an untrained puppy. Say, "Down, tongue, down. Relax! At ease!" Now, with jaw and tongue completely relaxed, say, "la, la, la, la, la, la," as if you were a drooling baby. Your tension soon will drool away.

4. The Yawn. Yawning is a number-one relaxer for the throat. With eyes gently closed, bring your lips together lightly. Drop your jaw loosely, lips still closed. Let a great big lazy yawn take over, opening your mouth and the back of your throat w-i-d-e; feel the stretch, up and sideways, of the muscles, opening the throat.

If, as you yawn, you look at the back of your throat in a mirror, you will see the uvula pull up and shorten like a rising curtain. That is the way it opens to make way for sound. In all speech, except when you are saying "m," "n," or "ng," your throat should be open. To feel the difference between a closed and an open throat, say, "ng-ah, ng-ah, ng-ah," several times. On the "ah" sound, the throat is completely open. On the "ng" sound, it is completely closed. You want the sensation of the open throat.

5. Speak the three sentences below. First place the palm of your right hand flat on your chest under the collarbone, feeling chest resonance and vibrations on those bones. You should not have any nasality because there are no nasal consonants in any of the words.

- The girls giggle over at the wall.
- All four stores are out of stock.
- Orchids cost a lot. Daisies are cheap. Violets are sweet.

MUMBLING, SPEED-TALKING, AND CHOP-TALKING

1. For lazy-lips, here are some alliterative sentences of "w" words. Pronouncing the "w" makes your lips a megaphone and gets them working.

- Why do working women wonder whether they will be winners?
- Walter woefully whiled away the weeks when Wilma went West.
- Weeping willows waved wanly in the wailing, whistling wind.
- Wanda walked wearily and watched Watson washing windows.

2. Say the polysyllabic words below slowly and smoothly, stretching them out. Support strongly with your vital triangle and give an extra tuck-in of support on the accented syllable.

apprópriately	nonrepresentátional
dispensátion	quíetude
propríetary	theorétical
monosyllábic	whimsicálity
polysyllábic	predestinátion
perpendícular	cantánkerous
valedictórian	fertilizátion
magnánimous	individualístic
beáutiful	libertárian
perspicácious	overwhélmingly
heréditary	regénerative
maníacal	unforeséeable

3. This drill is helpful for speed and chop talkers as well as for mumblers. Swing through each phrase smoothly, stretching it to make it last longer.

planning to	want to go through
planning to think	want to succeed
planning to buy	want to think well
planning to see	want to buy a lot
planning to do	want to see enough

going to win	want to be in style
going to improve	going to say more
going to lose weight	going to impress them
going to speak well	going to accomplish it

Now glide right through from beginning to end of each sentence:

* I'm planning to call because I need to speak with her.

* He will be asking for a contribution and I may not be ready to give it.

* She's going to do it if we want her to design the whole thing.

* We're planning to go to the office to see if we want to have a meeting.

* They're going to make reservations because they will be there next month.

* If we want to do it no one is going to stop us from seeing it through.

* We intend to leave if they're going to persist.

* Are you going to acquiesce even though you are against the idea?

* If I'm going to make a speech I want to enjoy doing it.

* Why don't you dress appropriately if you want to get ahead in business?

FOR MORE FLOWING SPEECH AND BETTER PACING

These exercises will help you with pacing. If you're a speed talker, drag out the phrases; if a slow talker, tighten them up.

1. First say each capital-letter phrase by itself on one flowing breath. Then say two phrases, with their connecting words, on one flowing breath. Then say the entire sentence, flowing smoothly.

* (He was) RUNNING VERY FAST (as he) WENT AROUND THE BEND.

* (He was) RUNNING VERY FAST AS HE WENT AROUND THE BEND.

* HE WAS RUNNING VERY FAST AS HE WENT AROUND THE BEND.

Say the following sentences in the same fashion:

* (He will) TAKE THE PLANE (and) GET THERE EARLY.

* (I shall) GO TO THE STORE (and) DO MY SHOPPING.

* (We like to) PLAN A GOOD VACATION (and) ENJOY EVERY MINUTE.

• (You must try to) LOOK TO THE FUTURE (and) PLAN FOR YOUR NEEDS.

• (He ought to) STUDY THE COMPANY (before) MAKING EXPENSIVE SUGGESTIONS.

• (She said) "IF I AM GOING TO ENTER THE MARATHON (I really expect to) BE ABLE TO WIN."

2. Read the following, concentrating on finishing each phrase smoothly, giving the "ring of truth" to each sentence:

• When the heart weeps for what it has lost, the spirit rejoices for what it has gained.

• I do not suppose that anyone here harbors illusions about the international prospects for the next few years. The barometer is falling.

• This situation requires wisdom, judgment, vision, persistence, and restraint.

• Compare what we all have to gain with success to what we all have to lose with failure.

3. Read the following sentences for projection, clarity, and pacing— the first time as though you're speaking to a small group in a meeting, the second, as though you're making a speech to a large crowd in a hall and there's no microphone. No mumbling. No nasality. Energize with the vital center. To avoid sounding singsong or tentative, go down in pitch at the ends of phrases, including the ends of questions.

• "Who's got the energy? We do. Let's use it to revitalize the economy. Let's use it to make ourselves heard. Let's use it to restore confidence, to build and to prosper. We have the need and we have the will to join together to fight for energy resources and the jobs they will create and keep. I don't know if we have any other choice. Like old age. It may not be the best of conditions, but it's better than the alternative."

—PETER J. BRENNAN

• It's easy to understand why nobody listens when we talk, why people don't believe anything anymore. How can we know if we are making the right judgment?

• A situation like this demands strong minds, courageous hearts, abiding faith, and ready hands.

• Language is the instrument through which we convey meaning to one another. Language is what differentiates us from the lower species.

• We need dreamers, thinkers, doers—we need you!

• "Many great civilizations in history have collapsed at the very height of their achievement because they were unable to analyze their basic problems, to change direction, and to adjust to the new situations which face them, by concerting their wisdom and their strength."

—KURT WALDHEIM

LISPING AND SIBILANCE

The "s" is more frequently distorted than any other consonant. At one extreme it becomes a "th"; at the other, a piercing whistle. Often a lisp is so slight its owner doesn't know he has it. It is easy to check. Simply say, slowly and distinctly, "Essential hospital nursing services." If your tongue touched your teeth or gum ridges on those "s's," you were lisping whether or not your ear caught the "th."

The following will help you get over lisping.

Sit straight in a chair; drop your head back loosely so that you are looking at the ceiling. Let your tongue fall back in your throat. In that position, with your teeth loosely together, hiss out loud. Aim a thin breath stream through the opening of your two upper front teeth, close to the gum line. The tip of your tongue should point to, but not touch, your upper gum ridges. Anchor the sides of your tongue lightly to your upper side teeth, furrowing your tongue lengthwise.

Return your head to its normal position, keeping your tongue retracted. Now read aloud from the list of words below. First say the word that starts with "t." Then say, out loud, "Retract the tongue." Pause, keeping your tongue retracted. Finally, say the word beginning with "s."

tame	"retract the tongue"	same
tub	"	sub
tell	"	sell
tip	"	sip
tight	"	sight
toe	"	sew
tot	"	sot
tat	"	sat
too	"	sue
told	"	sold

The sibilant "s" often occurs because of a gap between two front teeth, either upper or lower. It is like the whistling sound of a teakettle. It can be an irritating sound.

If your "s's" whistle, you need to put interference in the way of the breath stream. Instead of retracting your tongue as you would to prevent a lisp, let your tongue tip touch the lower teeth and blow the "s" lightly over it and the lower lip. Try almost to lisp. Say the words below. First, say the word beginning with "th." Then say, "Think breath on tongue." Finally, say the word beginning with "s."

thin	"think breath on tongue"	sin
think	"	sink
thank	"	sank
thaw	"	saw
thong	"	song
thick	"	sick
bath	"	bass
worth	"	worse
truth	"	truce
forth	"	force

READINGS FOR PRACTICE

Speak the following excerpts aloud several times. Add more color each time through the variety of the five P's: pitch, pacing, projection, phrasing, and pauses. First mark the text with a pencil, as we suggested in our Code for Coloring in Chapter 4.

Let the word go forth from this time and place, to friend and foe alike, that the torch has been passed to a new generation of Americans . . . Let every nation know, whether it wishes us well or ill, that we shall pay any price, bear any burden, meet any hardship, support any friend, oppose any foe to assure the survival and the success of liberty . . . And so, my fellow Americans, ask not what your country can do for you; ask what you can do for your country.

—JOHN F. KENNEDY

The proverbs of all nations, which are always the literature of reason, are the statements of an absolute truth without qualification. Proverbs, like the sacred books of each nation, are the sanctuary of the intuitions. That which the droning world, chained to appearances, will not allow the realist to say in his own words, it will suffer him to say in proverbs without contradiction. And this law of laws, which the pulpit, the senate, and the college deny, is hourly preached in all markets and workshops by flights of proverbs, whose teaching is as true and as omnipresent as that of birds and flies.

—RALPH WALDO EMERSON

Everyone has inside of him a piece of good news. The good news is that you don't know how great you can be! How much you can love! What you can accomplish! And what your potential is!

—ANNE FRANK

Flowers have an expression of countenance as much as men or animals. Some seem to smile; some have a sad expression; some are pensive and diffident; others again are plain, honest, and upright, like the broad-faced sunflower and the hollyhock.

—HENRY WARD BEECHER

You took the good things for granted. Now you must earn them again. For every right that you cherish, you have a duty which you must fulfill. For every good which you wish to preserve, you will have to sacrifice your comfort and your ease. There is nothing for nothing any longer.

—WALTER LIPPMANN

There seems to be something in the human psyche that makes years ending in "9" or in "0" important. In the "9" ending years, we tend to look back and assess where we have been. In the "0" ending years, we tend to look forward to see where we're going. Both are fascinating exercises and both assume that there is something magical about an artificial construction called a decade. But the future *is* important. The Cheshire Cat in *Alice in Wonderland* said: "If you don't know where you want to go, it doesn't much matter how you get there." I would only add, "If you don't know what the road is like, you can't get there at all."

—LOET VELMANS

Thinking cannot be clear till it has had expression. We must write, or speak, or act our thoughts, or they will remain in half torpid form. Our feelings must have expression, or they will be as clouds, which, till they descend in rain, will never bring up fruit or flower. So it is with all the inward feelings; expression gives them development. Thought is the blossom; language the opening bud; action the fruit behind it.

—HENRY WARD BEECHER

Let's tell them that the victory to be won in the twentieth century, this portal to the golden age, mocks the pretensions of individual acumen and ingenuity. For it is a citadel guarded by thick walls of ignorance and mistrust which do not fall before the trumpets' blast or the politicians' imprecations or even the generals' batons. They are, my friends, walls that must be directly stormed by the hosts of courage, morality, and of vision, standing shoulder to shoulder, unafraid of ugly truth, contemptuous of lies, half-truths, circuses, and demagoguery.

—ADLAI STEVENSON

We are a nation of many nationalities, many races, many religions—bound together by a single unity, the unity of freedom and equality. Whoever seeks to set one nationality against another, seeks to degrade all nationalities. Whoever seeks to set one race against another, seeks to enslave all races. Whoever seeks to set one religion against another, seeks to destroy all religion.

—FRANKLIN D. ROOSEVELT

Neither let us be slandered from our duty by false accusations against us, nor frightened from it by menaces of destruction to the government, nor of dungeons to ourselves. Let us have faith that right makes might, and in that faith let us to the end dare to do our duty as we understand it.

—ABRAHAM LINCOLN

Where, after all, do universal human rights begin? In small places, close to home—so close and so small that they cannot be seen on any map of the world. Yet they are the world of the individual person: the neighborhood he lives in, the school or college he attends, the factory, farm, or office where he works.

Such are the places where every man, woman, and child seeks equal justice, equal opportunity, equal dignity without discrimination. Unless these rights have meaning there, they have little meaning anywhere.

—ELEANOR ROOSEVELT

It's a little out of season, but I'd like to talk turkey today. Two questions. Are you getting tired of being taken to the cleaners? Are you getting upset because we have been fighting a defensive battle, and we came in second? Let's start thinking and acting like people who mean to win. Let's ask ourselves what we have to do to be number one again.

—FLOYD DEVEREUX

If you had a choice, would you rather be run over in the middle of the road by a steamroller going forty miles an hour, fifty miles an hour, or sixty miles an hour? Think about it. Take your time and discuss it. Because that is exactly the kind of debate that's going on throughout business today. We are standing—all of us—in the middle of the road watching a steamroller of laws and regulations bearing down on us. It's just about to flatten us, and all we talk about is whether it's gaining speed as it approaches, or maybe slowing down just a bit. It isn't going to make a particle of difference. The end result will be the same. Whether it hits us going forty or sixty miles an hour, or backs over us while we're looking the wrong way—it is going to prove to be just as fatal.

—PAUL McMULLAN

What can a man do to move along in some kind of grace through his days and years? Well, there are a million ways of putting it, but it always comes to pretty much the one way—he can do his best, in accordance with his laws, and in keeping with his truth, in favor of himself, and on behalf of his expectation, to see it all through in the best possible style, with some meaning, and without harm to anybody else.

—WILLIAM SAROYAN

Let me leave you with this Chinese definition of happiness: May you always have someone to love, something to look forward to, and something that you care about to be involved with every day.

If you put into practice some of the hints in this book, you may make this definition of happiness a reality for yourself.

SUGGESTED REFERENCES AND OTHER AIDS

For the Public Speaker:

The Encyclopedia of American Facts and Dates, 7th Rev. Ed., ed. by Gorton Carruth, et al. New York: Thomas Y. Crowell Co., Publishers, 1979.

Funk and Wagnalls Standard Encyclopedic Dictionary. Chicago: Funk and Wagnalls Inc., 1965.

The International Encyclopedia of Quotations. Garden City: Doubleday & Company, Inc., 1978.

Newnes Dictionary of Dates, compiled by Robert Collison. London, England: Newnes Publishers, 1961.

On Writing Well: An Informal Guide to Writing Non-fiction, William Zinsser. New York: Harper & Row Publishers, Inc., 1976.

Speaker's Treasury of Anecdotes About the Famous, James C. Humes. New York: Harper & Row Publishers, Inc., 1978.

2,500 Anecdotes for All Occasions, ed. by Edmund Fuller. New York: Avenel Books, 1980.

Writing That Works: A Practical Guide to Writing Memos, Letters, Reports, Speeches, Résumés, and Other Business Papers, Kenneth Roman and Joel Raphaelson. New York: Harper & Row Publishers, Inc., 1981.

Periodicals:

Forbes, "Thoughts on the Business of Life" (list of notable quotations appearing in every issue).

Vital Speeches of the Day. Southold, N.Y.: City News Publishing Co.

Cassettes:

Executive Speech Audio Cassette Album, Dorothy Sarnoff. New York: Speech Dynamics, Inc., 1980.

"Presence Is Power" Video Cassette, Dorothy Sarnoff. New York: Speech Dynamics, Inc., 1980.

For Adding to Wordrobes:

Barron's Vocabulary Builder: A Systematic Plan for Building a Vocabulary, Testing Progress and Applying Knowledge, Rev. Ed., Samuel C. Brownstein and Mitchel Weiner. New York: Barron's Educational Series, Inc., 1978.

Dictionary of Synonyms and Antonyms, Joseph Devlin. New York: Popular Library, 1977.

Roget's Pocket Thesaurus. New York: Pocket Books, 1976.

30 Days to a More Powerful Vocabulary, Wilfred Funk and Norman Lewis. New York: Pocket Books, 1975.

Word Power Made Easy, Norman Lewis. New York: Pocket Books, 1979.

For Pronunciation:

N.B.C. Handbook of Pronunciation, 3rd Ed., compiled by James F. Bender, revised and enlarged by Thomas Crowell, Jr. New York: Thomas Y. Crowell Co., Publishers, 1964.

Pronunciation Exercises in English, M. Elizabeth Clarey and Robert J. Dixson. New York: Regents Publishing Co., Inc., 1963.

Words Most Often Misspelled and Mispronounced, Gleeson and Colvin. New York: Pocket Books.

Index